WITCH

Partner

Materialize Your Ideal Partner

MariLiza Backstrom

Brazil - UK - USA

ISBN 978-0-9859319-3-3 (Hardcover)

ISBN 978-0-9859319-1-9 (Paperback)

ISBN 978-0-9859319-2-6 (eBook)

Design & Cover by Christer Backstrom @ ChristerDesigns.com

Special discounts available for purchase in bulk for premiums and sales promotions, as well as for fund-raising or educational use. Special editions or book excerpts can also be created to specification.

For details, contact Special Sales by e-mail to: Info@WitchPartner.com

Published by I.A.M. - Inner Altitude Media

www.WitchPartner.com

We can bring the author to your live event.

For more information or to book an event, send e-mail to:

Info@WitchPartner.com

Published in Brazil, UK, and USA.

--- V 10 ---

First release: 12/12/13

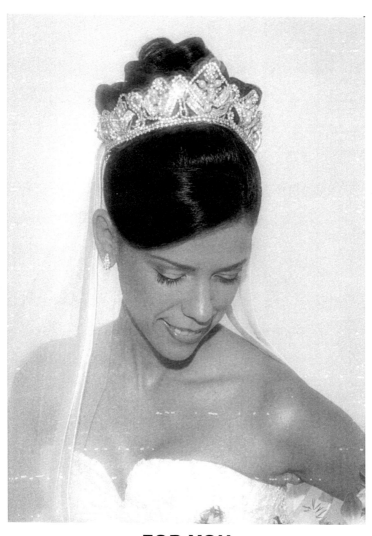

FOR YOU
who wants to
MATERIALIZE YOUR IDEAL PARTNER
&
HELP OTHERS
along the way.

THE PRELUDE
WARNING! KEEP ILLUSIONS AT BAY!

WHAT ARE YOU LOOKING FOR?

A: Your other half?

A: Your prince?

A: Someone to make you happy?

B: A complete person?

B: A real person?

B: Someone to share your happiness?

IF YOU CHOSE "A": *Uh-oh!*
If you believe you are a "half of a being"...
then it's time to become your whole self.
If you believe in "princes", then find a monarchy to
live in, or fairy tale to read.

If you believe that it's someone else's job to make you
happy, then find your fairy godmother or a genie.

Been there, done that and got bad results!
In my personal and professional experience, this approach
has brought more "frogs" than princes, more heartaches
than happiness and more illusions than results. So if you
want a new proactive approach to attracting a better
partner, then join us to create and implement your plan B:
the partnership plan.

IF YOU CHOSE "B": Wohooo!

WITCH PARTNER's readers are whole, real and happy with
their life. They just want to:

Share their happiness with a wonderful partner, or
Build a great business with a reliable business partner, or
Help someone who wants a great partnership.

DANGER: WISHFUL THINKING!

What do you really want in your ideal partner?
Be careful what you wish for, because you might get it.

If you don't wish what you really want, you might regret
once your wish is granted, because it might be too little or
too much.

Don't wish for more than you can handle!
Don't wish for less than you deserve!
WISH for what you REALLY want!

> Not to impress someone,
> Not to compare with anyone, and
> Not to show off as a trophy.

Be totally honest with yourself & with your partner!

WISH for what your heart truly desires; even if people tell
you that what you want is impossible. I've heard it many
times, but it never stopped me and here I am to show you
the great results. Wohooo!

WHICH
PARTNER?

11

IF
YOU
can

IMAGINE
your
GREAT
PARTNER,
you are
half way there.
The other half is to
ACT AS IF
you are there
ALREADY.

THE PREMISES

According to my beloved Master JESUS CHRIST:
"Ask and it will be given to you;
 seek and you will find;
 knock and the door will be opened to you.
 For everyone who asks receives;
 the one who seeks finds; and
 to the one who knocks, the door will be opened."

If you believe in his loving message, then
WITCH PARTNER invites you to:

ASK & BELIEVE
with CONVICTION that it's possible,

SEEK & BEHAVE
with DETERMINATION to see it through, and

KNOCK & BESTOW
with PRINCIPLES that will not allow you to settle for less.

THE EFFECTIVE STATE OF THE JOURNEY
Instead of focusing on how much it's going to cost, and
how long it's going to take, focus on how much you
will ENJOY THE JOURNEY, and how long you will LOVE
YOURSELF.

It's about loving the process, not the end product.
It's about self-discovery, not self-predicament.
It's about self-love, not self-luck.

Before our journey to attract your ideal partner, let's
gather the 3 essential for the partnership plan. I call it the
ABC essentials:

1. YOUR ASSET

Are you a great ASSET to your future partnership?

Do you LOVE & RESPECT yourself?

If you don't love and respect yourself as a great asset to the partnership, how can you expect others to love and respect you?

If you are not quite "there" yet in loving & respecting your precious self – Yes! You're precious! – then you might benefit from reading my first book, **_WITCH BEAUTY,_** where I share my true story from beauty victim to Beauty Victory and my journey to learn how to love and respect my self-image. There are ways to boost your self-esteem, choose what appeals to your values, style & mission in life.

Remember! It takes two to tango!

So before looking for someone to "dance", make sure you are in the same "level" as you wish your partner to be. The wonderful partnership you want starts with YOU. First and foremost, BE your best partner in your life. Do you enjoy your own company?

If you are "there" already - loving and respecting yourself – WITCH PARTNER will assist you to attract your great partner - like yourself - for:
life, business, or anything your heart's desire.

2. YOUR BELIEF

Do you have your TRINITY KEY?

Trinity key is what I call an essential triple belief system to achieve anything in life. In this case the Trinity key is customized to attract your ideal partner.

The Trinity Key:

1 - It's POSSIBLE to have a great partner!

2 - You CAN attract your ideal partner!

3 - You DESERVE to have a wonderful partnership!

3. YOUR COMMITMENT

Do you have TIME for your ideal partner?
Do you have daily time to find, get and keep your ideal partner?

Do you have RESOURCES for the journey?
Do you have space in your life for your ideal partner?

Do you have PERSISTENCE to design, develop and deliver your ideal partnership?
Are you going to continue if difficulties or doubts arise?

**Wishing & Working
Wonders
Worldwide**

THE REVELATIONS

WHY is WITCH PARTNER relevant?

- Is LIFE BETTER with a GREAT PARTNER?
- Is BUSINESS EASIER with a RELIABLE PARTNER?
- Do you want WONDERFUL PARTNERSHIPS in your life?

No?
Do you know someone who wants a great partner?
Would you like to help him or her?

Yes?
Then you already know why having great partners is a
very relevant topic. As you are here now reading WITCH
PARTNER, it means you are already manifesting your
desire to create better partnerships for your life and to
help others along the way.

It's crazy to expect to get a better partner, if we continue
to believe and behave the same way, over and over again.
Right? So this book helps you to break the vicious cycle
and achieve much better partnerships in your life or in
your business.

WHAT is WITCH PARTNER?

- A TRUE STORY from bad relationships to great
  partnerships,
- A POWERFUL PARTNERSHIP PLAN to manifest, measure
  and maintain wonderful partners in your personal,
  professional, or proactive life,
- MORE than a dating kit: it's a platform for relationship
  transformations.

HOW does WITCH PARTNER work?

By tapping deeper into your power of co-creating great relationships. You will learn how to:
• PROMOTE your persona,
• PRAISE your partner,
• PLAN your partnership actions to maximize your results.

WHEN to use WITCH PARTNER?

Whenever you want to:
• MATERIALIZE a great partnership, like: a love partner, a business partner, workout partner, or any desired partnership,
• EMPOWER someone who suffers with bad relationships,
• TRANSFORM your partnerships.

WHAT makes WITCH PARTNER unique?

This is an action based, goal oriented method; a practical guide to use your inner power and Universal Laws in your daily life to materialize your ideal partner.

WHO is MARILIZA BACKSTROM?

• SURVIVOR of bad relationships.
• CREATOR of great partnerships worldwide.
• W.I.T.C.H. who has transformed her life, materialized her own Vikingtastic partner, and shared her successful secrets in 11 countries.

WHAT are the pillars of the WITCH PARTNER method?

- PERSONA - BELIEVE in yourself as a great partner,
- PARTNER - BEHAVE as if you already have your ideal partner, and
- PARTNERSHIP - BESTOW the fruits of your partnership

**My partnership journey distinct phases:
Ouch, Wohoo, and Om!**

THE TRANSFORMATION

As most romantic girls, I spent many years of my life dreaming about my first love, marriage and *happy ever after*.

Of course, I expected to be like my parents and grandparents who had been together all their lives until they passed away. The unwritten rules of relationships were that you could date a few people, but when it came to marriage it had to be just once in a life time.

Without blowing my own horn, my single life was great. No problems in meeting & dating men – quite the contrary – and I have a lot to be thankful for. I am considered to be – even by my own standards - intelligent, attractive, and successful. I fervently love people, but I was rarely *in love* with people. What I loved first and foremost was true friendship, but many times my male friends fell in love with me, which ended up breaking the friendship, and my heart. I loved them as friends, but I was not in love with them.

Once my first marriage fell apart after 2 years of long & lonely struggles, I was completely depleted with a devastating feeling of failure, which pushed me from the edge of myself into the darkness of a terrible depression. To make things worse, I was so ashamed to be dragged to a psychiatrist, to take medicine and to go into therapy. How could this honored "A" student go so wrong in the relationship department? Marriage seemed to be so easy for everybody else - what happened to me?

When I first looked back on my partnerships journey, I got overwhelmed! Oh My Great GODDESS!

When it came to relationships, I had it all: from terrible to terrific!

If my partnership journey was a piece of music, it would go from heavy metal, to a romantic ballad, and to new age. It could be represented by 3 distinct phases: Ouch, Wohoo, and Om!

Let me give you a glimpse:

OUCH! TERRIBLE RELATIONSHIPS

• TORMENTED by jealous boyfriend
I had my first kiss, love and heart break with my first boyfriend. We dated for 9 years and the first 5 years I was tormented weekly by his raging jealousy. **Inconceivable what low self-esteem can do to someone.**

• USED by exploiter husband
I married someone very different from me: culturally, financially and spiritually. After a year dating and 2 years married supporting him financially all the way, it took me 6 years to divorce him as he tried to fight in court to get alimony from me. **Unbelievable how low a man without honor can go.**

• ABUSED by dishonest relatives
I was invited to be a business partner by two of my closest male relatives to build houses. Each partner would have a third of the company. I worked really hard for 6 years to save & send money to them and later found out that they were robbing me in many ways. They used my money, abused my trust, and never added my name to the company's deed. It was the worst betrayal as they were the people I helped most throughout my life. I requested my money back to leave the company, but once again

their dishonest nature prevailed. They refused to sign a payment schedule and they never honored the 3 proposals they put forward. When I finally realized they were both very dishonest, I took the case to court, and even in court they lied. I won the case in court after 8 years waiting, and they continue to try to take advantage of the slow & corrupted justice in Brazil and to postpone for as long as possible giving me what is rightfully mine. **Unforgettable, the pain of being stabbed in the back by your own relatives.**

WOHOO! TERRIFIC PARTNERSHIPS

• LOVED by Vikingtastic Husband
When I told some friends that I was creating a partnership plan to find my ideal partner, they said I was crazy and that what I wanted was impossible. Thank GODDESS I was already an International Coach & Master Trainer, so I respected their beliefs, but kept the ones who would help in my journey. **Magical what we can achieve when we align the trinity power of believing, behaving and bestowing.**

• RESPECTED by Mindful Business Partners
Once I created my partnership plan for my love life and was successful in finding my Vikingtastic partner, I had an insight that other partners could be materialized the same way. WOW! Great! So I starting applying my partnership plan to finding my business partners, which created the opportunity to meet and work with people from different countries, as I desired.

OM! Transcending CONNECTIONS

• ONE with ALL & ALL with ONE

Since I achieved my goal to have a Vikingtastic Husband, some of my friends started asking for help, after that my clients, and then the workshop was created. The more I use and share my partnership plan connected with my spiritual path, the more clear is the realization that we are all connected - even with the people we have not met yet. Our energy vibrates around the world and through different dimensions affecting everyone and everything. Once we embrace that inevitable truth, we become more responsible for our Wonders, Wishes, and Works. Any resemblance to the World Wide Web is not a mere coincidence. If we didn't know then, you must know now. We are One, and One is All.

My loving partnership could never be achieved if I didn't love & respect myself first. Learning to embrace my body as a divine temple and creating my secrets for beauty transformation was an essential pre-requisite to materializing my ideal partner. In my previous book *WITCH BEAUTY,* I share my 10 secrets for beauty transformation so anyone can feel beautiful in any age, size and shape.

My partnership journey was not such a straight smooth line as I had expected, but since I've learned to expect the unexpected and to appreciate the ups, downs, twists and turns of the emotional roller coaster of relationships, the ride has been more enjoyable than ever before. This book is my invitation to you for the ride of a lifetime. You can co-create your desired life and materialize your ideal partner.

Yes! I am a W.I.T.C.H. and so are you if you so wish!

My personal symbol is a flying W.I.T.C.H. (Woman Inspired Transcending Concepts of Humanity), but not because I practice WICCA, which I have the utmost respect for.

It's my personal reminder that we all have the power to transform our lives and help others along the way.

Whenever I want, I transform the meaning of the acronym to whatever best empowers me in each situation I have to face. No matter what meaning I choose to use, the purpose is always to be a reminder of our power to transform and transcend beyond the chains of limiting beliefs.

Ready...to **MATERIALIZE** your ideal partner**?**
Set...to **CO-CREATE** your desired partnership**?**
Go...& **COMMIT** to your own happiness**!**

One of the most spiritual places I have ever
been in my life: Jokhang Temple.
Lhasa, Tibet.

**The most sacred, yet forsaken journey
is the one within.**

**What are the walls of your sacred
inner temple saying?**

THE JOURNEY

We all want the delicious fruits of life and love, but we can't have the fruits without the roots. It's the principle of sequencing.

So my Trinity Partnership Plan — The P3 Plan — is on three strong "roots" (pillars) so your "tree" (partnership) can grow stronger and give you the fruits you wish.
The Trinity pillars create a platform for transformation to materialize your ideal partner for love, business or any partnership you desire:

1st Pillar - THE PERSONA – The Sacred Temple (You)
It's a journey of self-awareness through the seven powerful vortices of your existence: The Chakras
Self-mastery is the key to great partnerships. People say:
" *Love yourself before you can love others".*
I totally agree, but you can not love yourself without knowing yourself first.

2nd Pillar - THE PARTNER – The Special Guest
It's a process of co-creation through the Universal laws represented by the seven Hermetic Principles.

3rd Pillar -THE PARTNERSHIP – The Social Event
It's a bridge of effectiveness through seven successful business strategies.

THE PLATFORM

The structure of the Trinity Partnership Plan.

PART I – THE PERSONA – The sacred temple
1. *THE PATTERNS*   *The marks on your temple*
2. *THE PLEASURES*   *The entertainment at your temple*
3. *THE POWER*   *The control at your temple*
4. *THE LOVE*   *The care for your temple*
5. *THE FREEDOM*   *The rights in your temple*
6. *THE AFFILIATIONS*   *The public in your temple*
7. *THE CONNECTION*   *The higher purpose of the temple*

PART II: THE PARTNER, The Special Guest
1. *THE MENTALISM*   *Where it all starts.*
2. *THE CORRESPONDENCE*   *The dimensions that matter*
3. *THE VIBRATION*   *Through time & space*
4. *THE POLARITY*   *The archetypes*
5. *THE RHYTHM*   *The timing*
6. *THE CAUSE & EFFECT*   *The action*
7. *THE GENDER*   *The Yin & Yang*

PART III: THE PARTNERSHIP, The Mutual Agreement
1. *THE PROACTIVITY*   *The Attitude*
2. *THE EXTREMES*   *The Start & End*
3. *THE PRIORITIES*   *The Management*
4. *THE BENEFITS*   *The interactions*
5. *THE COMMUNICATION*   *The message*
6. *THE SYNERGY*   *The Flow*
7. *THE ENHANCEMENT*   *The improvement*

My invitation is to you is:
Embrace yourself mercifully
& co-create yourself masterfully.

With my favorite guards.
Rajasthan, India.

Are your partners guarding or guiding you?

THE TRACKS

While I was designing my partnership plan to materialize my ideal love partner, I realized that I had to take a serious look at my relationships – past and present – to learn about my patterns of choices and behaviors through the years. I needed a good inventory of what I had learnt from each relationship and the effective & ineffective patterns in my life. Of course, to take inventory of old stuff in my love closet was not something I was looking forward to at all.

In Brazil, when I was a teenager, my friends and I used to call our "ex boyfriends": THE GHOSTS! They were "dead" to us, but sometimes they came around in our mind and heart to "haunt" us. And oddly, I was about to invoke the "ghosts" from the tombs in my past. Ai! Ai! Ai!

Revisiting old wounds was definitely not what I wanted, but like a bitter medicine I had to inoculate myself with a wise vaccine to protect myself from future relationship diseases. In my opinion, suffering without learning is a waste of time – or it's for masochists. Pain is certainly not my "cup of tea", so I had to learn something useful from the good times, and especially from the bad ones.

Creating a time line with the major former partners (real or platonic) would help me to have a better overview of what I was doing "right" and "left" in my relationships. I drew a horizontal line on a piece of paper, and on that line I chose locations to represent past, present, and future. Magically, as if emerging from the depths of my heart, each ghost ("ex" partners) who touched my life (platonic or not, physically or not) rose to the paper and sat on the time line staring at me.

They each positioned themselves on the time line according to the time I met them. The first ghost was my first boyfriend when I was 15 years young in Brazil. We dated for 9 years. WOW! Such a long time!

The second ghost was my second boyfriend when I was 26 years young in the UK for a few months. The friendly and unfriendly ghosts kept emerging from the paper into the time line until all the former partners of my love story emerged.

Oh My Great GODDESS! I was totally shocked with the results! WOW! What was I *thinking*?

Some ghosts were friendly and brought a smile to my face, but others gave me the creeps. How could I ever have let those creepy guys get anywhere near me?

It was hard to believe that at some moments of my life my self-esteem must have been so low, in order to allow myself to get anywhere near these type of guys and situations. Phew! I was disgusted with some of my choices in the past, but immensely relieved that they were in the past. Phew! THANK GODDESS!

Looking back made me realize how many unnecessary risks I took through dangerous situations by not standing up for myself and my principles. The danger surrounded me whenever my "self" was vulnerable, missing my "esteem".

I was scared by the realization that despite being strong in most circumstances in my life, in other moments I was extremely weak and nobody ever noticed; not even myself.

If I really wanted to move forward to a great partnership,

I had to be totally honest with myself and take inventory of all my weakness. I had to face the names of every man that had touched my mind, body and spirit, even if it was just platonically!

Such a simple exercise, yet extremely powerful. It was just a piece of paper with a horizontal line and a few names, and yet it gave me all sorts of wild feelings. The horizontal line became a roller coaster of emotions. I was shocked, embarrassed, angry, sad, disgusted, happy, confused, emotional, anxious, and other feelings I could not even describe. It was very overwhelming! As if my mind was shouting, I heard my mind criticizing me: loser, slut, weak, naïve, clingy, stupid, dreamer, crazy, and mostly heavy insults. I went to both extremes of the self-esteem spectrum; from the highs of being loved & respected to the lows of being used & abused.

Noticing that I was getting into a downward spiral of emotions, I stood up, looked up and breathed in deeply. After focusing my attention on a few deep breaths, my muscles started relaxing and I got back to a calmer state. **A piece of paper was not going to kill me; however my self judgment could.**

Looking back at the paper, this time I chose to dissociate myself by looking at the time line as snapshots of the movie of my relationships, where I was the main character. Choosing to take the director's role in my life allowed me to change the genre of my movie anyway I wanted. I could look at my relationships movie as drama, thriller or comedy, with a simple shift in my mind. I could choose whatever "genre" that made me feel better, more comfortable and have a clear vision. **Strong emotions can blur our understanding and make us too reactive instead of productive.**

What was needed was to look at my partnership stories from a place of compassion towards myself. As a coach I had mastered some of the strategies to dissociate and ground myself as an observer, instead of the victim, the villain, or the judge. I called this position the "director's chair" and it required two things:

- **DISSOCIATION**

By looking at my story as if I was watching a movie in which I was the main actress, I could be referred to in the third person: *She*.

- **COMPASSION**

Acknowledging the efforts and good intentions of every character and every actor in the movie, and deciding that whether they were good or bad actors, they all gave their best shot according to the knowledge and resources they had at the time.

Once I started using this powerful director's position, I looked at myself as the main character and referred to myself in the third person (*She*). This trick helped me to keep emotions at bay by dissociation, which resulted in better understanding about the character and the actress (in this case myself). The actress should not be judged - nor defined - by the role she had been playing. After a while, I could clearly see the plots that my character got herself into and the reasons why she had been so vulnerable and trapped in those plots. It was a weird feeling of seeing myself as a whole different being, for the very first time from a respectful observer point of view. Each relationship that my character had been through gave me a better understanding about myself. **It was tough to realize first hand how much I took myself for granted. Ouch!**

As if I was pushed to fall from the director's chair, an emerging pain burst into my chest. Once again, I was sliding back to my "role" on the time line and getting caught up in judgments and emotions. As I realized my own trap, I heard myself saying: *"Change your position, find your comfortable director's seat, breathe deeply in and out a few times!"* After a few minutes regaining my balance, I went back to the director's seat, and I was OK again.

This first contact with my timeline helped me:

- **ACKNOWLEDGE**
All the parts & partners in the movie of my life,
- **PRACTICE**
The director's perspective from where I can change the genre of the movie, and to show
- **COMPASSION**
Towards all the efforts and good intentions of every actor in the movie of my life.

At this point this was all I wanted to achieve. It was not so easy, but it was totally worth it. **I felt like a veil had been lifted and I could see myself clearly from a place of acceptance and compassion.** As I had learned to keep the judgments and emotions at bay, I could look from a wiser point of view, and notice the conscious & unconscious patterns in my love life. Only from this position of dissociation & compassion, I could clearly see the successful & unsuccessful strategies I had used to find, get and keep my love partners.

What was freaking clear was that my great relationships came from times when my self-esteem was strong, and my painful relationships came from the times when my self-esteem was weak.

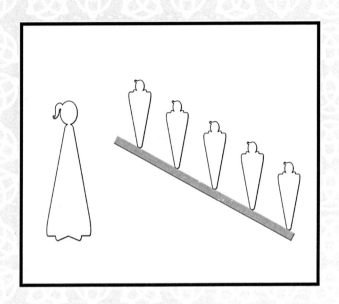

Who are the main characters of your love stories?

Which beliefs and behavioral patterns emerge?

THE PATTERNS

You can use a Timeline as a powerful tool to gain awareness about anything you want. Focus in the partners who have touched your life, in a good way or not, platonically or not.

Create your "Partners Timeline". It will give you a better overview of your partnerships through time and space. Keep dissociated from an observer perspective when looking at the roller coaster of emotions.

The director's position is even better than the observer's position, because the observer can only watch the "movie", but the director can "change" the movie as desired. In the director's chair you gain more insights of how to transform your partnership life the way you want, by modifying your thoughts, feelings and actions.

The idea is to bring awareness to the past experience, and gain knowledge about the triggers of vulnerability. Be as serious or as silly as you wish.

CREATE YOUR TIMELINE EXPERIENCE:

● THE TIMELINE
Draw a horizontal line on a clean piece of paper and write the location for Past, Present and Future. Then choose a location to add your current age on the Timeline.

● THE PARTNERS
Who are the partners that touched your life - mind, body or spirit - in a good or bad way? Add their names or initials of your Timeline in the order as you met them, from childhood to adulthood.

● THE AGES

At which ages have you met those partners? On top of the horizontal line, add the ages in which you met each of those partners.

Once you have drawn your Partners Timeline, it's time to reflect upon it. This second part is very important, and it requires what I call:

ACCESSING YOUR ABC WISDOM

ASSUME POSITIVE INTENTION

Embrace the premise that behind every action there is a positive intention. People, including yourself, do the best they can, with the power, knowledge, and beliefs available to them at the time. This premise is the key to creating compassion toward yourself and others, which gives you power to create long-lasting partnership transformations.

BE IN CONTROL

Imagine yourself sitting in a director's chair, looking at your Timeline as if it was a movie. As the director of this movie you have the control to watch it in any way it appeals to you. You can speed it up or slow it down. You can even change the genre of the movie. It can be drama, thriller, horror, romance, comedy or anything you like.

The director's chair is a metaphor to a dissociated position where you can watch any roller coaster movie without being caught up in the emotions of the ride.

As a director you have the control to give new meaning to past chapters of the movie, and also create new exciting chapters in the present and in the future. You can not change the facts and people in those scenes, but you can change the tone and the meaning of any scene.

CREATE A NEW SCRIPT

Enrich your life with the awareness of the turning points in your journey from a director's perspective. Notice from your past experiences:

MOMENTS   When & Where

- When did you meet your partners?
- What was your mood when you met them?

INFLUENCERS   Who & What

- What relationships (platonic or not) impacted your life?
- What did you learn about yourself in those relationships?
- What situations helped or hindered your self-love?
- What did they do to help or hinder you?
- What relationships drained and energized you?
- What did you do to maintain and enhance your self-esteem?

STRATEGIES   How & How often
How can you do things differently from now on?
How often are you going to check if you are going toward your desired destination?

Based on the knowledge you acquired about yourself, you can create a new script for your partnership life.

- What patterns did you identify in your partnerships?
- What was the source of your beliefs and behaviors?
- Are those beliefs and behaviors helping or preventing you to achieve your desired partnerships?

Based on your desired partnership, you can tweak your current "script" until it is what you want.

What beliefs and behaviors can give you better options? What can you do to acquire those beliefs and behaviors? When and how are you going to do acquire each belief and behavior?

Write the answers in your Partnership Plan, start applying them and after a week check the initial results.

The danger surrounds us

whenever

our "self" is vulnerable,

missing our "esteem".

One of my favorite beaches.
Melbourne, Australia.

SOMETIMES
The Flesh is weak! Oh La La!
The Heart is soft! Ai! Ai! Ai!
The Mind is tricky! Oops!
The Spirit is vague! Shhh!

THE SENSATIONS

Throughout my life I always had close male and female friends. I really like to learn from the different perspectives of each gender.

My female friends cuddled my heart, and my male friends challenged my mind. The problem was that often, after a few years of friendship, my close single male friends ended up falling in love with me.

No! I didn't like it at all! Sure, it was a nice stroke on my ego, but I'd rather preserve the strong friendship than to risk it mixing up with other feelings.

Unfortunately, every time a male friend declared his love and realized I only wanted his friendship, the friend ended up distancing himself out of shame or sorrow. The distance broke my heart every time, but I kept going and making new friends.

My Partners Timeline helped me to remember those relationships and what I learned about sensuality & sexuality; love & sex.

Those relationships taught me the importance of knowing the difference between: "to love" & "to fall in love"; to have sex & to make love.

Pleasure & Love are vital elements in our lives, and yet most of us get them mixed up. **Sex pleasures the body. Love pleasures the heart.** Having both is a sublime ecstasy.

Later in life I've learned to add two more powerful

ingredients to that incredible explosion of pleasure: the mind & the spirit. And it became a "Divine Foursome": Body, Mind, Heart and Spirit.

Often people think that sex can promote feelings of: intimacy, healing, love, and commitment. However, when we assume gaining those feelings from sex alone, we most likely get disappointed, or we disappoint others.

On my Partners Timeline journey, I noticed one time when I was lost and hurt by the tragic loss of the most important person in my life. He was my idol, best friend, and the love of my life: My Amazing Dad Pedro.

When two irresponsible drivers raced on the streets of my hometown and killed my Dad instantly, I died with him. Everything I loved most in my life was taken away from me in a split second; all because of a driving game.

I completely lost my mind. Thanks to my spiritual beliefs, divine intervention and caring for my Mom's health, I chose to live. It was my way to help my Dad's piece of mind in the spiritual world, by taking care of myself and my Mom in the material world.

After 9 months helping my Mom recover from a bipolar crisis caused by my Dad's death, and after organizing everything about my Dad's work and estate, I took off, desperate to heal myself.

I didn't know at the time, but I was emotionally sick and extremely vulnerable in a way I had never been before. Nothing made sense, nor seemed to matter. I went on my round the world trip that I had already planned prior to going back to visit my parents. That was the only thing "on my plate" at that time so I just took it. I was 27 years young and had only dated and kissed 2 boyfriends in my life. The first boyfriend I dated for 9 years (on weekends as we lived in different cities) and the second for a few months (sporadically as we lived in different countries).

When I went on my 6-month round the world trip I had more casual dates with men than ever in my life. I went from one guy to the next, blindly looking for a safe port for my heart. I was lost at the sea of love.

I could not see it myself, but I was so emotionally hurt, mentally confused, physically weak and spiritually lost.

I was such an easy prey. I always met a lot of interesting men in my travels, but I never dated, hooked up or hung out with anyone. I knew that "traveling love" is very tempting and temporary.

But on this journey I was feeling so lost and lonely, that in a few months I ended up dating more than I had done in my whole life.

There is nothing wrong with people who date a lot, but I wasn't being myself. I was badly grieving my Dad's sudden departure. I was missing and longing for the source of love, fun and protection in my life. I didn't realize I was looking for it in all the wrong places.

After six months traveling I went back to the UK and decided to live there again. I needed as much distance as possible from Brazil and the horrible memories of my Dad's tragic death, and the plague of corruption in the Brazilian justice system.

There were witnesses who testified that the drivers were

racing on a regular avenue, causing the accident that killed my Dad instantly. The witnesses testified that the two drivers ran away, leaving the scene without helping my Dad. The drivers were never taken to jail, because they were from rich & famous families who could afford expensive lawyers and could get away with murder.

One of them is the son of one of the most famous Brazilian soccer players in history. Just the thought of my Dad's death being dismissed so easily because of money and power, left me feeling sick and disgusted. My need for emotional closure and shelter made me vulnerable to the core.

My Brazilian friend whom I met while working in Brazil was living in a studio in the UK and he offered me to stay with him. He was the typical Brazilian guy: crazy about soccer and flirtatious with women.

He always flirted with me, but I never took him seriously — after all he was a good friend of mine; like a brother. I trusted him and shared my struggles with my Dad's death and other issues. I cried on his shoulder so many times.

As a backpacker, who stays in dorms at youth hostels around the world, sharing dorms with other people is not a big deal. I didn't think anything about sharing a studio with my friend. We had traveled together many times and we always shared spaces. He had declared his love for me a few years earlier, but I told him at the time that I only liked him as a brother.

It was wonderful to see that he didn't go away from our friendship and he seemed to be OK with the fact that I was not interested in him as boyfriend material. Without my knowledge, our physical and emotional proximity created unrealistic hopes in his mind that this time I would accept his love. I told him again that this would never happen because I was not attracted to him in that way.

When I have a good friend it's like I don't perceive their gender. There is no difference between a female and male friend in my heart. He was always helping me and I really appreciated it. However I forgot that he was a man, in love with men and he had his own agenda, apart from being my friend.

He knew I loved foot massage, so he was always reaching for my feet and giving me hours of massage at home, parks and even at the cinema. But I should have known that this was not a "friend move"; it was more like a man trying to seduce a woman.

Unfortunately he ended up getting too close. It was horrible! A double feeling of regret took over me. The regret of being so emotionally weak to let him get so close, and the regret of creating an impossible hope in my friend's heart. The worst hit me hard when he said:

"MariLiza, you give strangers a chance to date you; why can't you give the same chance to a friend?"

Oh My Great GODDESS! How can I tell a friend, without hurting his feelings, that I was not and would never be attracted to him in the way he wanted? How can I say nicely that he is not my type whatsoever?

I tried my best to compliment all his qualities and thank him for his efforts, but at the same time, to be clear that there was no chance we would ever become a couple.

My Partners Timeline made me realize that twice in my

life I had fallen in the same "friendly" trap: letting a good male friend get too close as a boyfriend.

The first time, my friend and I were very naive and we both got hurt in the confusion.

The second time it was with a different male friend, we were both wiser and we avoided any confusion, we just enjoyed the moment.

There is no right or wrong when it comes to dating a friend. What is important is to be aware of:

>What are we doing?
>Why are we doing it?
>How are we affecting each other?

Sometimes, when we are suffering, our pain is so intense that we get blind to the harm we are causing ourselves and others in the process of trying to heal, survive or have pleasure.

The "grieving" state of mind can cause unnecessary extra harm. There are many reasons to fall into the "need of affection" mode:

>death of a loved one,
>loss of a job,
>fight with a friend,
>break up with a partner,
>betrayal,
>bullying,
>accident,
>low self-esteem, and
>other critical situations.

Watch out!

Sometimes we are too beaten up to stand,
so we grab crumbs.

Sometimes we are too insecure to choose,
so we let others decide.

Sometimes we are too blind to reach out,
so we keep in the dark.

Sometimes we are too proud to ask for help,
so we get overloaded.

Are you looking for Mr Right
or Mr *Right Now*?

THE PLEASURES

When we know our inner triggers of pleasure and pain, it's easier to find strategies to use them in our favor, instead against us.

What are you looking for right now?
        Love?
        Sex?
        Intimacy?
        Protection?
        Trust?
        Other?
        All the above?

What do you need from a partner right now?

What do you want from a partner right now?

Is "having sex" the same as "making love"?

What is the difference in our opinion?

Are you looking for "Mr Right" or "Mr Right Now"?

While looking for Mr Right, are you going out with Mr Right Now?

Are you trying to transform Mr Right Now into Mr Right?

Are you always honest with your partner or prospect partners about your intentions?

Is it possible to be in love with more than one person?

51

Is it possible to fall in love with a partner you previously have not been in love with?

When do you feel most:
       Loved?
       Sexual?
       Intimate?
       Protected?
       Trusted?
       All the above?

What can help you to achieve them?

When and how are you applying them?

Add the key answers and actions to your partnership plan, start apply them consistently, an check the results periodically.

"WATCH OUT!

SOMETIMES

The Flesh is weak! Oh La La!

The Heart is soft! Ai! Ai! Ai!

The Mind is tricky! Oops!

The Spirit is vague! Shhh!"

Stealing a kiss in a Temple.
Singapore

**Are you INVESTING
in your ideal PARTNERSHIP?**

THE INVESTMENT

While considering to take a new course — a PhD in Human Development — to add more skills into my career as Coach & Trainer, I realized something very important. We, human beings, are really "funny", to say the least. **We spend years investing daily in what doesn't matter and nothing in what matters daily.**

What I mean is...

M**OST OF US** invest a lot of time, money, and efforts in our CAREERS. We go to school, take courses & buy books. **MANY OF US** invest a lot of time, money and efforts with our BODIES. We work out, buy gadgets, go on diets, etc. **SOME OF US** invest a lot of time, money and efforts in our SPIRITUALITY. We pray, buy books, volunteer, etc.

My question is...**What do we do for RELATIONSHIPS?** The answer is...NOTHING!

When it comes to relationships, we leave it to "chance". We "bump" into people & think: "Let's see what happens."

In general, we invest:
NO TIME to understand ourselves, our desires & values,
NO MONEY to find & foster great relationships,
NO EFFORTS to plan & persist to co create great partnerships.
After bad relationships in my personal and professional life, which left me emotionally and financially depleted, one day I said to myself: "ENOUGH! It's time for a new approach & better results!"

55

Some people say:
"If it's meant to be, it will happen."
I prefer to say:
"If I make it happen, it will be!"
Others say: "God willing!", waiting for His work.
I rather say: "God is always willing for our work."

As I had enough of random bumps into the wrong partners, I said to myself: "It's time to put my sacred trinity - body, mind & spirit - to work and create a new approach to finding a wonderful love partner.

Not a boyfriend, not a husband, but a great partner to share my happy life with. And so I did!

The Power of self-awareness is essential and later leads us to expand the awareness about others. I started investing time, money and efforts to learn about myself, others and relationships.

RELATIONSHIP with MYSELF

I read books, took tests and paid attention to who I was and who I wanted to be. I started reading about different personalities, archetypes, communication styles, astrology and relationships. I took scientific & mystical approaches to having a bigger spectrum of wisdom. Some tests that I took were free and self-directed and others were for a fee and with assistance.
A few examples:

> MBTI – Myers-Briggs Type Indicator,
> KEIRSEY - Keirsey Temperament Sorter,
> RIGHT Brain vs LEFT Brain test,
> ARCHETYPES test,
> CHINESE astrology (Based on the Moon's cycles)

WESTERN astrology (Based on the Sun's cycles)
VAKOG - NLP's representational systems.

RELATIONSHIP with OTHERS

Knowing my own preferences and personality made it easier for me to understand why I got along well with some people and not so much with other people. The next step was to understand how to communicate better with people no matter what preferences or personalities they had. It was crucial to learn:

> conflict management technique,
> win-win solutions, and
> non-violent communication.

RELATIONSHIP with a HIGHER SOURCE

As a Creative Coach, I crafted solution-oriented and action-based techniques.
As a Transformative Trainer, I manifested new beliefs & behaviors to bestow partnership excellence.
As a Mindful W.I.T.C.H., I connected to GODDESS to expand my perception & guide my intuition.

The result was ASTONISHING!
It was much better than I could have ever wished for!
I THANK GODDESS everyday for allowing me to materialize my VIKINGTASTIC PARTNER since 2009.

I designed, developed and delivered my partnership plan to transform my personal life and now help others along the way. Since then, I have used the same powerful knowledge for other types of partnerships, like on my spiritual journey and my business relations. It's been a life changing experience!

**Are you competing or collaborating
in your partnerships?**

THE POWER

When we know our personality traits, it's easier to understand and manage our tendencies towards fulfilling our dreams. Knowledge, especially self-knowledge, is powerful & priceless.

Do you prefer to be with the wrong person rather than alone, or to be alone rather than with the wrong person?

Do you want to get married someday? Why?

Do you want to get married in the next 3 years?

If you get pregnant and you are not married, what would you do?

If you discover that your son or daughter is gay, what would you do?

What is your biggest fear about getting into a committed relationship?

What if you want kids but your partner can not have kids?

What if you want kids but you can not have kids?

Is it normal for physical attraction to fade over the course of a relationship?

Have you ever been tested for STDs?

Should you ever talk to your partner about STDs?
Would you consider dating someone from another:
race? country? age group? religion?

Reflecting in Prospect Park.
New York, USA.

Through which "lenses" should I see myself?

THE SELF MASTERY

It doesn't matter how rich, young, beautiful and famous we may be, we all have moments in life when our self-esteem is depleted and needs a little recharge. It's essential to live a healthy life – with or without a partner – to know how to boost our own self-esteem.

Self-esteem can be related to a number of aspects of our lives: body, mind, finance, health, youth, marital status, etc. It doesn't matter how many of those ingredients you use to "measure" your self-esteem; what matters is to know which ingredients you use and what you do in case you find yourself short in the balance.

In my first book "*WITCH BEAUTY – 10 Secrets for Beauty Transformation*" I share my true story of struggles & strategies to feel beautiful in any age, size and shape. It focuses on our sacred temple – our bodies – but you can use the same secrets to empower any side of your sacred temple: intelligence, skills, success, health, and the list goes on.

The key is to create your unique "EMOTIONAL EMERGENCY KIT" – the things you can do to recharge yourself when your self-esteem is running low. It's important to have a variety of "tools" in your bag so you don't get dependent on one person, one strategy or one situation.

The more I look into mine and my friends' dating experience, the more I see a clear pattern: **the better our self-esteem, the better our relationships.**

Since I learned this essential truth, I've guarded myself

from going out with a prospective partner when my self-esteem is vulnerable. Basically I said "NO" to invitations to go out with someone new when I wanted it the most. Crazy? Not really! Think about it!

Should you go to the supermarket when you are starving?
NO!

Should you go out with a prospective partner when you are starving for affection?
NOOOOOO!

If you do, what probably ends up happening is that you will show your "messy" side and sell yourself short. I've been there and done it. It's not worth it!

Our need of affection fools us into believing that it's better to have a little bit of attention – even from the wrong person - than none at all. It's more common than we want to admit. I've noticed over and over again that we all do it at some point, and especially women.

We want to fall deeply in love, but we don't want to fall flat in love. Do we?

Love is the most magical part of life. Falling in love is like being under a spell, everything around us is transformed and we hope that this spell will never end.

Love is something we like to share, but to share something we must first have it. Right?

If you want to love & be loved, first and foremost you have to possess the essential feeling:

SELF-LOVE!

How can you expect others to love you if you don't love yourself?

One of my personal mottoes is:

I don't have everything I love, but I do love everything I have, and this love satisfies me completely.

A healthy self-love unleashes two other essential tools to create "magic": self-respect and self-confidence.

If you don't respect yourself, why would others?
If you don't value your inner assets, who will?
If you don't trust that you have what it takes, why would others take the risk?

If you love and respect yourself, you will not let others manipulate, dominate and abuse you. You will stand up for your right to be treated well. You will set the example of how to treat yourself.

Others will get the message and treat you well or leave you well.

SELF-ESTEEM is the key to materializing
any healthy partnership you wish.

Even when you already materialized your ideal partner, it's essential to keep your self-esteem alive and well.

**Do you love yourself
unconditionally?**

THE LOVE

ASK YOURSELF:

Do you love yourself?

Do you respect yourself?

**Do you have self-esteem and pride
in your own being?**

Are you happy and healthy alone?

**Even when you don't have a partner, do you feel
secure in yourself and fulfilled in your life?**

Those who don't feel secure in their life, and are seeking to build their life around a partner usually can not detach from their desire to manifest a successful partnership.

They are locked in a love poverty consciousness, contracted by the fear of being alone.

If you are not happy alone, what steps must you take to gain a greater security with yourself and your own life before you find your partner?

Do you really want a partner?
If so, what kind of partner?

There are many ways to boost your self-esteem; here goes one my favorites that I started intuitively a long time ago, and later I realized it is practiced by my lovely Witches:

65

MIRROR MAGIC

When we look at any mirror, we have 2 choices of perspective: to look at what we don't like about ourselves, or to look at what we love about ourselves.

Guess which perspective leads you to self-love?

Just like brushing your teeth is good for your dental health, these affirmations are good for your self-esteem health.

You can add these affirmations as part of your daily health routine, like after brushing your teeth.

Make it your daily ritual to look in the mirror and *say out loud*:

I AM BEAUTIFUL!
I AM A DIVINE CREATION!
I LOVE you _____ (your name).
I AM proud of you _____(your name)!
You can do anything you want!
You are amazing!

LOVE ENERGIZERS

I LOVE Myself.
I LOVE Others.
I AM loved by GODDESS
(GOD, Universe, or whatever symbol you prefer)
I AM open to give & receive Love.
I FORGIVE myself.
I FORGIVE others.
I AM open to love and be loved in all dimensions.

Practice this loving exercise daily for 30 consecutive days and check the powerful results!

Wall Street Systems Analyst by day,
Professional Samba dancer by night.
USA & UK

**Embracing my authentic duality and
having fun in the process.**

THE AUTHENTICITY

At the top of my career as a Wall Street Systems Analyst in New York at the biggest bank in the USA, I had a very funny & curious boss for a while. One day I went to work with a small suitcase and when he saw it, he rushed to talk to me and pointed to my bag: *"Are you going to travel?"*

My eyes went to where he was pointing and I realized that he was curious because there was a colorful feather coming out of an opening on my luggage. It was clear he was trying to find out what I was up to, just like a little child excited to see a new package at home.

With a mysterious and naughty smile I said:
"Don't worry! I will be here tomorrow!". I walked away from my desk leaving him with a huge question mark on his face. It was funny to see him struggling not to invade my privacy any further by asking more questions. It was obvious that the curiosity was consuming him. Ha! Ha! Ha!

The next day I was at work in front of my computer, when my boss came rushing through the corridor, gasping with a newspaper in his hands. He stopped at my desk, sized me up and down, looked at me with startled eyes and pointing to a photo in the newspaper he asked: *"Is that you?"*

I looked at the photo of me as a professional samba dancer wearing a sexy costume performing with other dancers at a major event in Times Square – the heart of New York. As if having my photo in newspapers was the most natural thing. I said: *"Yes!"*

He looked at me and back at the photo a few times and he said: *"Are you a professional dancer? Do you perform regularly? Is that why you came with that suitcase yesterday?"*

With a proud smile I said: *"Yes!"*

He was so excited and astonished with my "double life" that he left day dreaming. A few hours later he came back to my desk and gave me the newspaper, saying: *"I went back to the newsstand and bought many copies: one copy for you and a few copies to give away. Is that OK?".*

I said seriously: *"Thank you, you didn't have to do that!"*

Knowing how much of a gossiper he was, I asked:
"Did you already distribute the other copies?"

Very embarrassed and blushing he said:
"Yes! Sorry! I was so proud of you!"

I said: *"You are very lucky that I am friendly and proud of being a Professional Brazilian Samba dancer, otherwise I could sue you for invading my privacy and spreading photos and info about my personal life without my previous consent. Next time ask permission first."*

Despite his misconduct, what surprised me the most was how shocked and amazed my boss was about e having an artistic side and being proud of it.

My Wall Street friends – IT geeks & Financial wizards – could not believe I was a professional samba dancer at night. My samba dancer friends could not believe I was a Wall Street Systems Analyst by day. My two worlds could not believe and come to terms with my personalities. My pride and joy was obvious when people saw my smile when they discovered my double life. I never hid it; I just never advertised it. This duality started at a very young age when I was a math "A" student, selected to represent my school in Math competitions, and also Figure skater in a big "Broadway-like" show in my sports club. Until my boss brought me the newspaper, all puzzled, I never realized that most people thought that it was weird to have a double life with parts so extremely different from each other. Suddenly, it struck me: If people could hardly handle one of my identities, how could I expect a partner to handle my two unique identities?

Since that strike of wisdom I understood that if I ever wanted a great partner in my life, he would never be the average Joe. Nope!

It had to be someone very special who would be excited to have someone with such different interests and lifestyle. I wasn't going to change my essence to "fit" into some "one dimension" partner. I didn't want someone who could cope with my dimensions, but rather someone who truly enjoyed them all. Someone who could enjoy the challenge of going from physical to intellectual in a second, from bullshit to spirituality in a snap, then back and forth again without losing the grasp of the matters. I know! I never said I was normal, nor did I ever want to be. Ha! Ha! Ha!

This reality check was essential on my journey to materialize my ideal partner. I discovered that in my life mirror there were always two images side-by-side. Not only was I proud about my "twins", but also aware of what they would require in terms of materializing a great partnership. My love quest was much more exotic and challenging than for most ladies. Most women want the tall, good-looking, rich, educated, single man, but I wanted was a combination much harder to find. The thought of finding this rare type of man did not make me scared; quite the contrary. It made me extremely excited! Wohoo!

One Man who could keep two very different ladies entertained and satisfied. Yes! A very "twinsted" threesome! Oops!

Many men fantasize about having a threesome, but most men can hardly make one woman really satisfied. Now imagine keeping up with two very different ladies all day and all night and share it all. Yes! What I wanted as a partner was very special; that is why I had to create a very special partnership plan.

This funny episode with my boss woke me up to the fact that there are so many people tied up in keeping up appearances that they never fight for the freedom to be their true self. I believe we are all diamonds with lots of interesting facets to be explored. I decided to double check my "facets" to find out if there was any "twin" missing from my inner team. Crazy? Maybe. Fun? Definitely. In any attempt made to describe and materialize my ideal partner I had to know all the facets of my own "twin" persona upside down and inside out.

On my quest to discover gems of knowledge and create my precious partnership plan, I wanted to give it my best shot so I unleashed my powerful twins for the challenge:

Mari - The Logic & Liza -The Magic

My best work always comes from the atomic fusion of embracing my polarities:

Left brain & Right brain = Mari & Liza.

It may sound crazy to you, but it makes perfect sense to me. A true Gemini is not a person who has two faces! Not at all. It's a person who has two distinct personalities. I may be a freak, and if so, I am freakily happy about it. Where people see competition, I see collaboration. Two brains think better than one. Where people sense craziness, I feel happiness.

All this to say that my twins researched through Heaven & Hell to find wit & wisdom to materialize my ideal partner.

Mari & Liza went in totally distinctive directions. Mari reached out to Science and Liza reached out to Spirituality. While Mari scientifically researched human behavior, Liza intuitively investigated ancient wisdom. Even though they have reached out to completely different sources of knowledge, funnily enough they came back with the same incredible gem: The Archetypes.

The importance and power of the archetypes have been present in Science, Religion, Business and the Arts for as long as human existence, and yet we rarely use this incredible source of power to understand the way we operate and what we want to achieve.

If you look at successful companies, most of them use archetypes to structure the brand identity and tap into their target consumer's inner desires to sell them products. If the successful companies study and apply this ancient wisdom for business, why couldn't I use it for love?

Are you letting your
true voice come out?

THE FREEDOM

We all take on patterns (archetypes) inside us. We may have a combination of a few archetypes, but in general one is predominant. It becomes our persona and the way we handle everything in our lives. When you understand your main archetypes, you will understand more about yourself and your ideal partner.

In general, we are comfortable with people like us — like our own archetype — and we are attracted to people that are opposites of us. With opposites there is more friction, but also more opportunities to learn from each other, like in a great team. Archetypes are universal symbols and show patterns of behavior. They are often used in myths and storytelling across different times and cultures.

STEREOTYPES are indicated by PHYSICAL ATTRIBUTES.
ARCHETYPES are indicated by PSYCHOLOGICAL ATTITUDES.
Archetypes are stronger & deeper than any stereotype ever will be!

Yes! Mind over matter!

Which are the strongest influences in your life?

Check the following archetypes and choose one that best represents you. Make a note of your archetype in your partnership plan, and check how it prevents you from, or propels you toward achieving your goal.

If you find that your personal archetype is creating some obstacles to achieving your goal, then what can you do to overcome it?

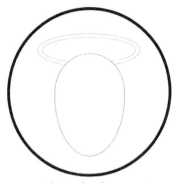

THE INNOCENT

MOTTO: Free to be you & me
DESIRE: to get to paradise
GOAL: to be happy
FEAR: to be punished for doing something bad or wrong
STRATEGY: to do things right
WEAKNESS: boring for all their naive innocence
TALENT: faith and optimism
The Innocent is also known as: Utopian, traditionalist, naive, mystic, saint, romantic, dreamer.

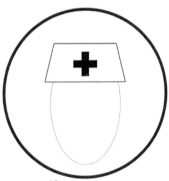

THE CAREGIVER

MOTTO: Love your neighbor as yourself
DESIRE: to protect and care for others
GOAL: to help others
FEAR: selfishness and ingratitude
STRATEGY: doing things for others
WEAKNESS martyrdom and being exploited
TALENT: compassion, generosity
The Caregiver is also known as: The saint, altruist, parent, helper.

THE REGULAR Guy or Gal

MOTTO: All men and women are created equal

DESIRE: connecting with others

GOAL: to belong

FEAR: to be left out or to stand out from the crowd

STRATEGY: develop ordinary solid virtues, be down to earth, the common touch

WEAKNESS: losing one's own self in an effort to blend in or for the sake of superficial relationships

TALENT realism, empathy, lack of pretense

The Regular Person is also known as: The good old boy, everyman, the person next door, the realist, the working stiff, the solid citizen, the good neighbor, the silent majority.

THE HERO

MOTTO: Where there's a will, there's a way

DESIRE: to prove one's worth through courageous acts

GOAL: expert mastery in a way that improves the world

FEAR: weakness, vulnerability, being a "chicken"
STRATEGY: to be as strong and competent as possible
WEAKNESS: arrogance, always needing another battle to fight
TALENT: competence and courage
The Hero is also known as: The warrior, rescuer, superhero, the winner and the team player.

THE EXPLORER
MOTTO: Don't fence me in
DESIRE: the freedom to find out who you are through exploring the world
GOAL: to experience a better, more authentic, more fulfilling life
Biggest fear: getting trapped, conformity, and inner emptiness
STRATEGY: journey, seeking out and experiencing new things, escape from boredom
WEAKNESS: aimless wandering, becoming a misfit
TALENT: autonomy, ambition, being true to one's soul
The explorer is also known as: The seeker, iconoclast, wanderer, individualist, pilgrim.

THE REBEL

MOTTO: Rules are made to be broken
DESIRE: revenge or revolution
GOAL: to overturn what isn't working
FEAR: to be powerless or ineffectual
STRATEGY: disrupt, destroy, or shock
WEAKNESS crossing over to the dark side, crime
TALENT: outrageousness, radical freedom
The Outlaw is also known as: The rebel, revolutionary, wild man, the misfit, or iconoclast.

THE LOVER

MOTTO: You're the only one
DESIRE: intimacy and experience
GOAL: being in a relationship with the people, work and surroundings they love

FEAR: being alone, a wallflower, unwanted, unloved
STRATEGY: to become more and more physically and emotionally attractive
WEAKNESS: outward-directed desire to please others at risk of losing own identity
TALENT: passion, gratitude, appreciation, and commitment
The Lover is also known as: The partner, friend, intimate, enthusiast, sensualist, spouse, team-builder.

THE CREATOR

MOTTO: If you can imagine it, it can be done
DESIRE: to create things of enduring value
GOAL: to realize a vision
FEAR: mediocre vision or execution
STRATEGY: develop artistic control and skill
TASK: to create culture, express own vision
WEAKNESS: perfectionism, bad solutions
TALENT: creativity and imagination
The Creator is also known as: The artist, inventor, innovator, musician, writer or dreamer.

THE JESTER

MOTTO: You only live once
DESIRE: to live in the moment with full enjoyment
GOAL: to have a great time and lighten up the world
FEAR: being bored or boring others
STRATEGY: play, make jokes, be funny
WEAKNESS: frivolity, wasting time
TALENT: joy
The Jester is also known as: The fool, trickster, joker, practical joker or comedian.

THE SAGE

MOTTO: The truth will set you free
DESIRE: to find the truth.
GOAL: to use intelligence and analysis to understand the world.
FEAR: being duped, misled—or ignorance.

STRATEGY: seeking out information and knowledge; self-reflection and understanding thought processes.
WEAKNESS: can study details forever and never act.
TALENT: wisdom, intelligence.
The Sage is also known as: The expert, scholar, detective, advisor, thinker, philosopher, academic, researcher, thinker, planner, professional, mentor, teacher, contemplative

THE MAGICIAN
MOTTO: I make things happen.
DEISRE: understanding the fundamental laws of the universe
GOAL: to make dreams come true
FEAR: unintended negative consequences
STRATEGY: develop a vision and live by it
WEAKNESS: becoming manipulative
TALENT: finding win-win solutions
The Magician is also known as: The visionary, catalyst, inventor, charismatic leader, shaman, healer, medicine man.

THE RULER

MOTTO: Power isn't everything; it's the *only* thing.

DESIRE: control

GOAL: create a prosperous, successful family or community

STRATEGY: exercise power

FEAR: chaos, being overthrown

WEAKNESS: being authoritarian, unable to delegate

TALENT: responsibility, leadership

The Ruler is also known as: The boss, leader, aristocrat, king, queen, politician, role model, manager or administrator.

Chinese inspiration.
Beijing, China.

**Where or Whom do you reach to find
support in your journey?**

THE ALIENS & ALLIES

While working on my partnership plan for my love life, some people have asked what type of Man I wanted and without any hesitation I've given the highlights of my ideal partner.

What surprised me the most was to see their body language and unspoken message. Their comments didn't at all match what their body language was saying. Since I've learned to read people's energy field, it became even easier to "read" the truth between the lines. Often people's comments were supportive towards my desire and description of my ideal partner, but their body and energy were saying something totally different. Their reactions were different, and yet their message was the same. The message was clear:

In their body, the tension comparing their love lives.
In their mind, the disbelief in my power to succeed.
In their energy field, the disdain toward my right to achieve it.

Even one of my closest friends in New York who love to "play cupid" said: *"MariLiza, what you want is impossible!"* Thank GODDESS I was already an International Coach & Master Trainer to understand her good intension and her limiting beliefs, so I just replied:
"I understand you believe it's impossible, but I believe it's possible. If I exist, someone like me can also exist."
My friend looked at me with a mix of pity & disbelief. On a few other occasions while talking with me and other single ladies, she said that I was her biggest challenge when it came to finding a suitable match. By the way, I never ever asked her to do it. She used to tell other

friends, in front of me, that what I wanted was impossible. Those remarks were unnecessary and hurtful. I never ever asked her or anyone to find me prospective partner, nor to set me up with anyone. Actually I never liked that at all. There is nothing wrong in setting people up on blind dates if — and *only if* — the two people involved are interested in this kind of approach. I understand the good intention behind it, but it's just not my "cup of tea".

As I like to keep an open mind about new approaches, I did once accept an invitation from my hairdresser to meet her friend, but it was an intellectual disaster. I valued her good intention, but I think her only selection criteria was that we were both single and good looking. If she had investigated a little more she would know that there was never a chance that her friend and I would be a good match. Most people who like "playing cupid" think it is enough to know the parts involved, but to know someone doesn't mean to know someone's desires & dreams.

We may never know why people believe in what they believe, but we know for sure which beliefs propel us toward our goal and which others prevent us from achieving our goal. If I'd chosen to hold my friends' belief that the type of man I wanted was impossible to find, then what would be the chances of me finding him? Very small indeed, because deep inside I would be sabotaging myself.

So when working on my partnership plan, I chose wisely not only people who believe in my quest, but also who were wiling to support me along the way.

My witty & wise Dad used to say: *"Tell me who you hang with, and I'll tell you who you are."* His message of wisdom was echoing in my ears. Inspired by my Dad's wisdom I created my quote to achieve my goal:

**"Tell me what you want,
and I'll tell you who to hang with."**

What I mean is that you can choose to be surrounded by:
"Aliens" - People who believe & behave away from your goal, or
"Allies" - People who believe & behave toward your goal.

It is your choice and it makes a HUGE difference to the probability of you achieving your goal. Why? Because in our journey, there are those days that we feel weak and doubt ourselves and in those days the Allies cheer us up to get back on track.

I am not saying that you can not do it on your own. Sure you can! What I am saying is that it's better to have Allies along the way, and keep Aliens at bay. Adding another of my Dad's favorite quotes:
"Water dripping day by day wears the hardest rock away."

Even the strongest will eventually wears off when surrounded by people discrediting your beliefs & dismissing your behaviors. Watch out! As much as I loved my friend who said my wish was impossible, whenever I was "doubting" myself, I avoided her company and reached out to people who empowered me. I kept going hopeful and doing my part, then...

MAZAM!

And just like magic, here I am sharing my successful love story with you and others who want to materialize a great partner for love, business or any other partnership.

For each journey to make your dream come true, choose wisely your Allies, and recognize the Aliens along the way.

**Are your crowds
bringing you up or down?**

THE AFFILIATIONS

My P3 plan works only in the highest frequencies of energy, like compassion, forgiveness, gratitude and all the spectrums of unconditional love. That's why I don't say "Enemies". I don't believe in Evil, Enemies or Entities that represent fear. I choose to call Allies & Aliens because Aliens are not good or bad; they are just different. It's up to us to choose what the difference means. When we choose to clean our heart of the traps of fear, we reach higher levels of consciousness which manifest what people call miracles. I prefer to call it materializations.

The magical part of P3 plan is to work on the spectrum of love - The highest & Strongest level of energy in the Universe.

Of course, I am not perfect, and sometimes I get hurt and my heart holds some resentment, but as soon as I can I clean up my heart from those heavy feelings and start rising up to the higher level of love again — where all the amazing transformations happen. Most of us operate for far too long on the lower levels of fear, so to rise up to the highest levels of love we need to expand awareness, beliefs and compassion.

From your higher self, answer the following questions. When it comes to your journey to materialize your ideal partner:

Who are the ALIENS in your journey to materialize your ideal partner?

What could be the Aliens good intention behind their belief or behavior?

Can you respect their beliefs and let go of any anger or resentment toward them?

How can you clean your heart from those feelings?

How will you best handle Aliens if they show up in your "weak" day?

Who are your ALLIES?

How to reach out the support of your Allies when you need most?

What else can support in your journey? Allies can be books, movies, friends, quotes, songs or anything that lifts your spirits.

"Tell me what you want, and

I'll tell you who to hang with."

Reviewing my life's purpose on my favorite spot.
Austria.

What is my purpose in this life?

THE PURPOSE

As a Business Systems Analyst in Wall Street, or as a Business Coach around the world, I've learned the importance of defining clear Vision, Mission, Value and Goals, not only to create successful companies, but also to create successful partnerships in love and in business.

We can learn a lot from successful love stories and also from successful business stories. We may have different archetypes in different sides of our lives, but we can check which ones are more effective for each stage of our journey to materialize our dreams. The better we understand what moves us forward, the better we can inspire ourselves to keep going.

I've learned a pretty cool & a little scary exercise that takes us to another dimension. I was supposed to imagine my own funeral and figure out what people would remember me by and write on my tombstone. Would the way they see me be the same way I see myself?

Am I doing what it takes to leave my desired legacy? It's kind of freaky to do this exercise, but extremely powerful to bring us a complete new overview of our lives.

I realized that without knowing I had started moving toward my mission in life by changing my career. I am very grateful to my former career as a Systems Analyst which brought me to many countries and to live in USA, but I suddenly knew more than ever that it was just a career; not a calling.

As an International Coach, my true calling is to help people to believe in their divine potential to materialize their dreams and facilitate their journey. Only when I started studying and working as a Business and Life Coach I realized what it meant to truly work with love and love the work.

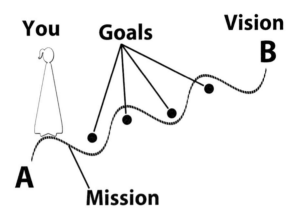

So the "death" exercise helped me to realize I needed to clarify my vision, mission, values and goals and align my life according to them. The partner was not my life goal; he would be a guest on my journey towards goals in life.

I did my homework and asked myself a question to clarify my life's journey in order to leave my desired legacy behind.

VISION –> desired future
Why do you do what you do?

Vision defines a desire in the future and it has no deadline.

What do you want to see in the future?
What is the future you seek to create?
Whose vision is it? Yours? Parents? Friends? Society?

What craving do you want to satisfy?

Where are you heading with your life?

If you could develop exactly the kind of life you want, what would it be like?

MISSION –> motivation behind vision
What do you do?

Why does this matter?

Working with Purpose and Meaning.

Why are we doing this?

Brings out purpose, motives, intention.

> * Why does this work [our work] matter?
> * What's most important about this work?
> * What will it do for us to fulfill our vision?
> * Why do our goals matter?
> * What is our unique role?
> * How do we "make a difference"?

For whom? How will we benefit? Who else benefits?

What's vitally important about our work? Begins to identify the values and interests that drive the organization.

With what aspects of this work do I most identify? Is there a cause or purpose — the bigger picture — beyond the work itself?

VALUES –> guide actions
How do you do it?

Which values am I living with today and where are the biggest gaps? As mentioned previously, it is often useful to define governing, core values, principles, or beliefs for the organization. What's the difference? Core Values underpin the organization's purpose and mission. Values might be reflected in words like teamwork, contribution, excitement, communication and quality. Once a list feels complete, go back and write a sentence that defines what each value means to you or to the organization.

Principles such as being "in service" to each other like internal customers (value: respect), win-win (value: success), or shared power (value: inclusion) have been central to successful corporate cultures.

GOALS – What steps do you take?
A common mistake is to establish goals and objectives without first defining the "container" — the vision, mission, and values that underpin that mission must be evident.

Goals and objectives are essential (*"If you don't know where you are going, you could wind up anywhere!"*), but vision, values, role definitions, and systems of tracking results all serve as the "container" for effective growth and development, and must first be put in place.

ROLES – What is your "costume" for the journey?
Who does what? Which are the key responsibility areas?

Once listed, be sure to define what they mean to you and to your future partnership.

"Without vision we are blind,

Without a mission we are lost,

Without compassion

we are sorry,

Without a goal

we are dead alive."

What will be your legacy?

THE CONNECTION

FOR THE BELIEVERS!

What if GOD uses relationships to shape you, would you see yourself differently?

1. If your actions left a footprint in this world, what would it show?

2. Would others want to follow your tracks?

3. If God loves you, do you love him back through your life?

4. If relationships are meant to shape you, what form & size have you chosen for your heart?

5. If God gave you an unique gift, do you share it with others?

6. What if spiritual gifts weren't about Holy Spirit juju magic...would that affect how you served the body?

7. What if you were really allowed to dream...would you dance, sing and create?

8. What if you really lived your passion...would you use it to change the world?

9. What if excellence really matters, would you use it to the challenge?

10. What if you could live like a traveler, would you shed your tourist self?

FOR THE NON-BELIEVERS

1. If you die today, what do you think people would write on your tombstone?

2. What would you *like* to see on your tombstone?

3. Are the messages similar?

4. If not, what can you change in your thoughts, words and actions to achieve your desired legacy?

5. What is your desired Vision for the world in the future?

6. What is your Mission in this life to contribute towards your Vision?

7. What are your Values that guide you in you Mission?

8. What is your role throughout your Mission?

9. What are your Goals?

Once you answer those fundamental life questions, go backwards in your note book where you have written steps for your partnership plan and re-evaluate how your life's purpose modifies the steps you have written before.

"Believe wisely,

behave wholly,

&

bestow worldwide."

Transforming my sorrows into wisdom.
São Paulo, Brazil.

THE MIND

Have you ever met someone working too hard to meet a partner? I have, and it's a sad sight, and most of the time the person doesn't even realize it. When people are desperate, it's very unlikely they will find a good partner for a healthy relationship. Potential partners will sense it and be turned off by it.

Whether someone wants a long or short term relationship, it's essential to have an attitude of contentment. One's appreciation for one's life has to come first and foremost.

It's also crucial to be more than just OK when one is alone. To be alone does not mean to be lonely. I have learnt the hard way that being alone and being lonely are two very different things. The loneliest time of my life was when I was married to my first husband. I was married and slept with someone next to me every night, and yet I felt like the loneliest woman on earth.

We can be in a crowd and feel lonely. We can be alone and feel great! This shows that loneliness has nothing to do with having people around us. We can choose to be our own best partner 24/7 and carry this healthy inner partnership with our higher self anywhere anytime. This inner partnership resonates deeper and further than any outside partnership ever will.

**"The All is Mind" -
"The Universe is Mental"**

Kybalion

THE MENTALISM

It's time to use your most powerful machine — your mind — to create a clear description of your ideal partner. Get a new page in your notebook, and start describing your ideal partner (your goal) in as much clear detail as possible.

THE S.M.A.R.T.E.R. PARTNER

S SPECIFIC
WHAT exactly do you want in your ideal partner?
How is he/she different from what you already had?
M MEASURABLE
HOW do you know when you have achieved your goal?
What indicates that you are getting closer?
How will you measure it?
A ACHIEVABLE
WHO has control or influence over it?
Can you initiate, execute and finish this goal?
Does this goal depend on you?
R RELEVANT
Is this goal RELEVANT to your life right now?
How does this goal align with your vision, mission, values?
T TIMELY (set specific dates)
WHEN do you want to achieve this goal?
When are you going to start working on this goal?
How often are you going to work on this goal? When?
E ECOLOGIC
How does this goal IMPACT your life?
How does this goal affect family, work, health, friends?
R RESOURCES
What RESOURCES do you need to achieve this goal?
What resources do you already have?
What resources do you want to acquire?
How are you going to acquire them?

THE BETTER APPROACH
How do you get yourself into a state of mind to attract a potential partner?

FIRST BE ATTRACTIVE
Happy + Active (1st Pillar- Persona)

THEN BE PROACTIVE
Prominent + Active (2nd Pillar- Partner)

EXPANDING your power to transform with:

• GRATITUDE
Have a heart full of gratitude for all the good things you already have in your life: health, job, home, family, friends, and much more.

• RECOGNITION
Recognize the values of not being in a relationship:
- If your had a toxic relationship or a bad breakup, you need time to heal and get stronger first!
- If it has been a long time since your last relationship, then your appreciation for having a relationship will be great once it happens.
- If you are afraid to be alone, this time gives you the opportunity to learn how to overcome it. It will help you to not stay in relationships below your standards.

• MATERIALIZATION
Use your six senses to visualize in details your ideal and S.M.A.R.T.E.R. partner and partnership.
- Spend 20 minutes daily visualizing in your mind what your ideal partner looks like, personality, and the qualities of your relationship as if it's happening in the present. Experience it now with all your senses! This creates a powerful vibration to be matched with what you want.

When you do this exercise you communicate to the Universal mind (GODDESS/GOD) what you want to materialize in your life.
- If you stay on track enjoying the ride, then it is very likely that one day you'll suddenly realize that you're in the partnership you imagined!

THE WISER BELIEF
What you believe is what you focus on,
What you focus on is what you attract to your life.
Believe wisely!

If you believe you will never meet your ideal partner, then that is exactly what you will manifest in your life: more loneliness and scarcity. Watch out!

Sometimes we try to find a partner, desperately and aimlessly. Most people want to meet a new ideal partner that night, that week, or that month.

Desperation forces things to happen too fast and when we have no clear idea of what we want in a partner regarding appearance, personality, principles and mission, etc, then when we meet someone it's probably not a good match.

The opposite happens when we are calm and grateful for our life. As you are comfortable in our own skin, and have a specific description of your ideal partner in your mind through materialization, your partner is likely to appear. It normally happens when you least expect it.

Learning the essential dimensions of my ideal partner.
New York, USA

What parts are essential in your ideal partner?

THE DIMENSIONS

While returning to my single life, and on and off dating interesting characters, something was stirring up in my guts, not only about my ideal partner's looks, but especially about what he would be made of. Reflecting on the Lights & Shadows (Qualities & Challenges) of my past partners, I acknowledged without judgment what I've learned about myself through from each one. As I didn't have much experience with dating before my first marriage, I knew I needed to acquire more knowledge about relationships and experiences to practice co-creating wonderful partnerships.

Now that I was dating with all my senses open (especially the sixth sense), a whole new world was opening up in front of me. For the first time in my life — in my thirties — I was feeling like a teenager, excited with the "treasures" on the path of love. Of course, there were many "frogs" and obstacles along the way, too, but I chose to believe that they are there just to make the overall experience more interesting. For a long time, like most girls, I believed a loving kiss was "magical" enough to turn a frog into a prince. I even went as far as marrying a frog until there was no more denial, only the truth: **"Frogs are frogs, and forever will be frogs!"**

Frogs will never turn into princes, or anything worthwhile for my life. Lesson learned! From that point on, my "frog radar" was much improved and it became easier to spot them, even when they were disguised as handsome bachelors. I only got in touch with frogs when I was interested in having a laugh and nothing serious. After all we have to respect every species' qualities & limitations. **Frogs jump, but I'd rather walk! Ha! Ha! Ha!**

By the way, a sense of humor is an essential magical tool in your journey to materialize your ideal partner, and also important later, to keep your ideal partner. Don't take yourself or anybody else too seriously. It's not worth it and it makes things unnecessarily heavy. We can be responsible, assertive, goal oriented, successful, caring and all, and still have a sense of humor in our personal and professional life. Believe me, I had to learn to laugh at myself, and at my mistakes to survive the painful divorce from my first husband. As I was too good for my own good, since I was a little girl, it was not easy to look at some of my poor choices with relationships. Learning how to lighten up the mood was a tremendous turning point to go further and faster in my partnership journey.

SEX's UP & MIND's DOWN!

Back analyzing my past partners (platonic or not), I noticed that almost every time I dated someone new I found a new piece of my ideal partner puzzle. It was like trying new amazing things that you never knew existed before and realizing you could no longer live without it. I will explain better!

In the past I dated a Brazilian that was amazing in bed. Is it hot in here or is it just me? Ha! Ha! Ha! Yes! He had all the right tools, moves and stamina to make any woman beg for more. As I never had so much sex in my life, I was deliciously overwhelmed and quickly got used to the feast. I thought: "Oh la la! Here we go! But as he was a good "9" to my body, he was an absolute "0" to mind. He knew how to excite my body, but he bored my mind. He wasn't stupid, but culturally and intellectually he brought nothing to the table. My body was satisfied by my mind was starving.

I could happily keep up with his sexual drive, but he could not keep up with my cultural and intellectual hunger. I am in no way saying that I am better or worse than anyone, but our needs were very different. Sex was enough for him, but not for me. He was not graduated, and had no interest in studying anything. I was graduated with honors, love to study and I was planning to get a Ph.D. I had a solid career, traveled the world on my own, bought my apartment cash (no mortgage) by the sweat of my hard work; meanwhile he never traveled anywhere, he didn't have savings, he was not investing in any career, and he lived with his parents in his thirties. When he talked, his basic language and many grammatical mistakes hurt my ears. I must confess that he made me embarrassed in front of my friends with his poor vocabulary, incorrect syntax and shallow content. As he loved me, in his own way he put a red carpet for me to walk. In my need for affection after my Dad's death, I got used to his full attention, and closed my eyes for my intellectual needs which were never met.

This relationship lasted far longer than my mind could cope with.

MIND's UP & EMOTIONS' DOWN

The next partner was from Israel. He was intelligent and traveled a lot like me around the world. WOW! Two great qualities, so I thought: "Great! Now we are talking!". I loved to hear his stories about traveling, his strategies to build his business and his career plans. It was so refreshingly sexy to have someone who kept up with my intellectual and cultural interests and brought new things to learn. It was the first time I was very attracted by someone's mind. He kept my mind highly entertained, my body moderately happy, but...of course there was a "but" — and it was a big "BUT" in my opinion — he could not express his emotions at all! Unbelievable! His face was the same whether I was leaving or arriving. As we lived in different cities and we could only see each other on weekends, his expression on my arrival and on my departure meant a lot to me. Not only did his face not show any emotions, but his comments about me and about his feelings were a complete blank. He was incapable of showing his true emotions like *"I miss you."*, *"You are beautiful."*, and things like that. He was amazing with intellectual essays, but could not say one sentence about his feelings. I knew he liked me through his actions. He called me every day and always made arrangements to see me on weekends, but he could not verbalize any feelings. As in my Brazilian culture it seems so easy to express emotions verbally, I took for granted that any boyfriend of mine would be able to do it too. Once I asked him if he thought I looked good before we went out. His reply was: *"I don't need to tell you that you are beautiful. Plenty of men tell you that every day."* I was shocked with his reply and I said: *"Well, I don't date those men, I date you, so I would rather hear it from you."*

During the week, when we were apart, we talked on the phone (no social media or texting yet). Our conversations were intellectually exciting, but emotionally frustrating. When we were together I wanted more than good sex and great conversation, it was then that I realized that there was another important layer of my needs: emotional connection. Not only did I want someone who could be great physically and intellectually, but also emotionally.

He knew about his emotional limitation and he told me that this is the way he was and he was not going to change. He said he tried in other relationships and it didn't work. He said I should enjoy what he could offer. Once again, I stepped into the "Fairy tale", thinking that with time things would change, until one day my heart had enough and said: *"Wake up, MariLiza! He's never been emotional before in all his life, and he already told you. Why are you still thinking he will change? Wake up and smell the Brazilian coffee brewing — elsewhere!"*

So as I was more aware of my essential partnership levels of needs, it was clear that it would never work. We broke up and continue to be friends and even as a friend he could not show or verbalize his emotions. However, as a friend it was OK to deal with.

EMOTIONALLY LOADED & SPIRITUALLY OVERLOADED

The next boyfriend that came to mind was African American. I met him in one of the lectures at my spiritual center. We were talking with a mutual friend who introduced us and — Bam! The attraction was quite clear. We left the lecture together, and he invited me for dinner, then he walked me home. Even though I've always been very interested and engaged in spirituality, I've never been remotely attracted to anyone from any of the spiritual places I've been, so this one came as a total surprise.

As he was so much into spirituality like me, I didn't notice that my expectations of him were quite "Divine". Yes! I really lowered my guard completely from the very beginning, just because I met him in my spiritual center. I am not talking about sleeping with him on the first date on anything like that. I am talking about the fact that I put him right on a very high pedestal of trust from the very beginning and without knowing him.

So I thought: *"Divine! Now we are transcending!"*

113

Like me, he believed in GOD, and he totally understood me — something that most people could not — when I said I was a Christian Witch. In my experience, Americans freak out when I say it. They have no clue what I'm talking about and they are too scared to ask. So It was spiritually refreshing to meet an American man so open-minded about spiritually, and also so engaged in working in his spirituality. He totally got me in my most precious level: Spiritually!

What a joy to talk to him about my spiritual studies, and all sorts of mystical things that most people have never even heard of. I was floating in the clouds of acceptance and understanding. To make it better the other important parts (physically, intellectually and emotionally) were well represented too. Wohoo! So how could it go wrong?

Well, it did! His priorities, time and energy were totally compromised with building his new business and keeping up with his spiritual duties with *Santeria*. My great grandmother was also in his line of spirituality with demanding spirits, but she only performed her duties at the spiritual center twice a week. In his case it was doing a lot of spiritual practices every single day. I couldn't believe the number of rituals he had to "perform" daily plus the casual ones. WOW! I was spiritually knocked down! Plus he was kind of pushing me to become a full-blown medium, which I was definitely not ready for, nor wanting to embrace.

Being so near to his spiritual guides and spiritual work, my sensitivity grew (as he was also pushing for it) too quickly for me to handle. I really needed some help to gain control over the feelings and readings around me. It's like he wanted me to spiritually fly high, like him, but he was pushing me to the abyss to fly on my own, because he didn't have the time to teach me how to "fly" and get over the fears of the unknown. He even admitted that. His time was completely booked solid for the next few months, divided only between his business and spiritual work. There was no time for a girlfriend. He tried to "squeeze" me in now and then, but I really wanted more than he had to offer. His priorities at that moment were very clear: business and spirituality. Anything else — like a relationship — was secondary. Surprisingly, I didn't take it personally and totally respected his choices. There was no right or wrong; just different Priorities & Timing. I broke up with him in peace. A new important piece of my partnership puzzle appeared: time & timing.

Based on my dating experience, it was clear that I was slowly but surely finding the essential layers of my ideal partner. Every boyfriend I had was adding a new dimension to my understanding of what was essential in my ideal partnership. The definition of my ideal partner until then was too vague and now it was clear.

As I tasted the "champions" of Sex, Intellect, Emotions and Spirituality, it struck me that I didn't need a champion in one dimension, but rather a good representative in all dimensions. I didn't want someone to be 100% — A Champion — in just one dimension. No! I wanted someone with a good representation in each.

I am certainly not 100% in one dimension, so I didn't expect anyone else to be. However, I could not cope with someone who was a 0% or lower than 20% in any of my desired four essential dimensions in a partnership. Some people may have more or less essential dimensions in their life, but in my case it was clear: Physical, Emotional, Mental, and Spiritual were essential in my life, so my ideal partner would share those dimensions with me somehow.

I started describing on paper all the attributes I would like in my ideal partner for each of those dimensions.

Example of an initial draft of my Ideal Partner

Physically
Tall, handsome, with hair, beautiful smile, strong, good in bed...

Emotionally
Romantic, calm, happy, optimistic, good manners, considerate...

Mentally
Curious, open minded, intelligent, graduated, like to learn & read...

Spiritually
Believer, grateful, respectful, open minded to my Witch side...

Based on my findings, I had to make sure and include all the essential dimensions of my ideal partner *in my mind* in my visualization, so it would come true *in my life*.

"Find the layers of your interests and find your dimensions."

"As it is above, so it is below;
as it is below, so it is above"

Kybalion

THE CORRESPONDENCE

On a new page of your notebook where you are building your partnership plan step by step, write the answer for the following questions:

How would you describe your ideal partner?

How many "dimensions" do you see in your description?

What are the dimensions of your ideal partner?
(Example: Physical, Emotional, Mental, Spiritual, Financial, Social, Sports, Entertainment, etc.)

Is there any important dimension missing from the initial description? If so, what?

Now that you defined your ideal partner's essential dimensions, write the name of each dimension on a page as a column on your partnership plan. For each dimension you create a column, and then you start filling up each column with the descriptions related to that dimension. Add as many details as possible. Go for it!

In my case it was like this:

PHYSICAL   EMOTIONAL   MENTAL   SPIRITUAL

But you can have as many dimensions as you want. It's *your* ideal partner, so be true to yourself and write what really matters to you. There is no right or wrong. There is what you like and what you don't. FOCUS only on describing what you like. For example, instead of saying: *"I don't want a workaholic"*, you can say: *"Balanced life style"*, instead of saying *"non-smoker",* you can say: *"Health habits".*

The reason for that is that our subconscious mind only processes "images". It does not work with "negative" images. Let me explain. My dear reader, ***do not*** think about a cute little pink pig with a red bow on its neck.

What are you thinking of right now? Of course, the cute little pig with a read bow on its neck. That was just to prove the point that the subconscious does not process negatives. So keep all the descriptions of your ideal partner in the positive mode.

Describe in a positive way all the qualities you want in your ideal partner. The more, the merrier.

"Reality is

reflected by your beliefs,

propagated by your words

&

manifested by your actions."

Beyond the boundaries of time & space around the world.

THE TIME & SPACE

Thinking about the way I have lived up to this point in my life, I've realized that my logical mind had been the ruler of my decisions. Even though I have always believed in the power of the subtle energies around us, I never used them to achieve my goals. Suddenly I could not figure out why it took me so long to use such powerful energies — available around all of us. A veil was slowly lifted, and I could see that my love for logic took over my decision-making for far too long. As I wanted different results in my love life, I decided to take a different path this time, by using my mystical nature.

As if having awakened from a very long sleep, my intuition regained life and flourished. It started by learning the natural laws, then tapping into those subtle energies. I read a lot, practiced often, then slowly but surely I became more intuitive about those energies flowing within me and around me. It was interesting to notice how we emanate energy, how we receive energy and how we exchange energy all the time. This subtle energy dance occurs daily in everybody's lives, but most people are not even aware.

Those energies follow the natural laws of the universe, which exist since the beginning of time, but only now are people becoming more aware of them. Throughout my life, my inner Witch has always been interested in the esoteric & natural ways to a better life like: Chromotherapy, Flower therapy, Acupuncture, Reiki, Feng shui, Astrology, Tarot, Telepathy, Mediumship, Neuro-linguistic programming, Holistic healing, Cosmic Integration, to name a few. Even though I haven't practiced tapping into those energies, I knew they were present in my life daily.

123

SPACE INSIDE FOR MY PARTNER

One day I was looking in one of my books about Feng Shui and how the universal energy ("Chi") can flow and the different patterns of yin and yang. The idea is to maximize the harmony between the flow of Chi and that of the user to bring good fortune.

For me the Chi is not magic, it's logic! Everything in this world produces vibration. Some vibrations prevent us from moving forward, and other vibrations propel us further; pretty much like swimming upstream or downstream. The difference is that with Chi you can change the directions or speed of this energetic river.

I kept reading until it hit me. WOW! I looked around my apartment and noticed for the very first time that my apartment had too much female energy (Yin) and almost no male energy (Yang). My collection of Female Icons (Goddesses and Witches), the colors, the shapes, almost everything in my apartment had female energy, so it made complete sense to me that energetically speaking, there was no space for male energy in my home.

The balance between Yin and Yang was not in harmony. I was astonished! My apartment looked great and organized, but the energy flowing was in the opposite direction from my desire. My heart wanted the male energy of a partner, but my place had no space for it.

My collection of Goddess & Witches stood proud, but alone on the shelves. My furniture resembled the round shapes of a female body, but there was no male form to embrace them. WOW! All this time I thought I was living alone, but in fact I was living in a female sorority house, packed with "Yingesterone". Ha! Ha! Ha!

My home was not in any way the stereotypical girly place with stuffed animals, hearts, pink lace or anything like that, but still had all the female vibration crowding the place. Looking through the Feng Shui "lenses" of wisdom, I could clearly see why no male energy could move in here.

As soon as I acknowledged the fact, my next step was to make the appropriate changes in myself and in my place. As my budget was tight since I'd changed my career, all I was planning to do was to move things around and some "DIM" (do it myself) stuff. After excavating through the forgotten boxes in my closet, I found some good prospective partners for my Goddesses, Witches and Angels. A good number of Gods and other male artifacts from different countries were now pairing up with my Ladies. I didn't have enough male figures to pair them all up, but at least half of them now had great partners courting them. I could not help but smile at the thought of my own ideal partner coming up to meet me soon. Wohooo!

"*WAIT A MINUTE,*" my intuition screamed, "Remember to live AS IF you already have your ideal partner!'

My mind asked puzzled: "*What do you mean?*"

"*If your ideal partner was living here, what would be different? Whatever it is, make it happen now! The present is the only time that exists and the only time we can live, so live with your ideal partner now.*"

"WOW!" My mind was blown away with this time warp. I thought about it, and the first thing that came to mind was my closet space. "*Oh, No! Do I have to share my closet space now? Really? But there is no partner here yet!*"

125

This crazy inner conversation between my mind and my intuition happened in a split second, yet it seemed like forever, but I got it in the end. If I wanted a love partner to come into my life, there must be a space for him. It didn't matter if my place was small or big. The point was to find the space in my place, and especially in my heart. Time for some serious cleaning up!

One of my dreams, since I was a little girl, was to have my own room with a walk-in closet, and since I finally managed to have my small walk-in closet after so many years of working hard, it was hard to think about giving up a big part of it to an "imaginary partner". Ouch!

What was my intuition talking about?

> ***Make room for love, and it will come.***
> ***Make a nest for love, and it will grow.***
> ***Make a home for love, and it will stay.***

> ***LIVE AS IF YOU ALREADY LOVE, and***
> ***LOVE AS IF YOU ALREADY LIVE.***

After some inner struggles, I finally let go of my "sacred" walk-in closet space, and emptied 50% of it for my ideal partner, whoever he was, wherever he was. I chose 50% because that was the space I wanted to give to him and receive from him. It was also a metaphor for the ratio that I wanted in my partnership. This was one of the hardest parts for me to do in my partnership plan: to share my walk-in closet. Living with a half-empty closet space was a daily temptation to fill it all up with my stuff, but I kept remembering to "respect my ideal partner's space" as I wished he would respect mine.

TIME FOR A PARTNER

Throughout my previous career as an IT Systems Analyst I've learned a crucial lesson when it comes to maximizing time and efforts: Work smarter, not harder!

As I created my new partnership plan with the premise to be as effective as a business plan, I added important strategies to the plan, like time management, quality assurance, investment portfolio, follow-up, feedback, to name a few. Just like any good portfolio you don't want to put all your eggs in one basket. You want to spread your efforts around to raise your chances.

So I divided my time and efforts between:

INTERNET

In the beginning there was a kind of stigma that if you admitted that you went online to meet people, it was a sign that you were a loser who could not attract someone in person. That is very closed-minded perception! The internet is just another door — just like going to a restaurant or a bar; there are going to be some good people ,and some not so good.

ONLINE DATING TIPS

1. Your photo is everything
2. Your screen name, headline and profile need to pop up
3. Less is more when it comes to describing your partner
4. Experience a large site and also a boutique site
5. Master the search engine secrets to get more results
6. Use the Witch Partner P3 plan to focus on your wish

INTRANET
Meeting men was always easy, as I am friendly and like to talk to new people; men and women.

MIXNETS
There are so many possibilities to have fun and meet people in person: dancing, playing a game, going to the movies, speed-dating, concerts and so many other ways.

PLAN
Conduct your search as you would for a job. Shine your light first, and show your shadow later. There is no competition! You are unique, so create your unique profile and partner. In general, let men be men! They like to hunt and chase, and the more they chase, the more they value the prey. Don't get me wrong, there are exceptions to the rules, and it's OK too. By the way, dress to express yourself, not to impress others.

STATE
The best state to meet a potential partner is in places where you are comfortable, doing what you like, and with people who you trust. These places bring the best out of you as you are happy and relaxed. That is your best state to meet your potential partner.

"Believe wisely!

What you believe becomes

reality in your life. "

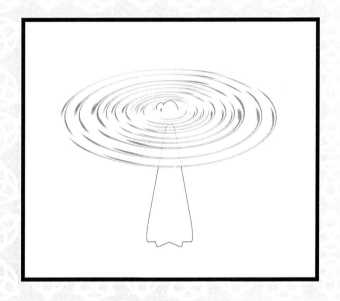

"Nothing rests:
everything moves;
everything vibrates"

Kybalion

THE VIBRATION

Vibrate toward your ideal partner through your thoughts, words & actions.

TIME FOR YOUR PARTNER
How much time do you want to spend with your ideal partner:

>   Daily?
>   Weekly?
>   Monthly?

How much time are you spending now to materialize your partner:

>   Daily?
>   Weekly?
>   Monthly?

Is the time spent on materializing your partner enough, not enough or too much?

Are you balancing the time between all the important things in your life?

SPACE FOR YOUR PARTNER
Do you have space in your life for the partner you want?

STATE TO MEET YOUR PARTNER
What are your biggest passions?
What activities make you excited?
What places bring you passion and joy?

Samba show.
London, UK.

Nothing is more liberating than being whatever you want, anywhere & anytime!

THE ARCHETYPES

One of the turning points in my life was when I had an epiphany at the amazing Leeds Castle in the UK. As if a dormant memory buried through many lives came to life. I realized that a long time ago in a different reincarnation I was a Witch in this land. It was a surprising, bitter sweet moment. I could feel the pain of discrimination, and the glory being myself, regardless what people thought or said.

Women suffered so much in the past and are still suffering at the present to have their Human rights respected. A big sigh came out of my chest as if a pressure from the past was released. A sense of pride and purpose started bubbling inside me with passion. From that day onwards my personal symbol of transformation became a Highflyer Witch. For some people it may sound like a contradiction to be Christian and have a Witch as a personal symbol, but for me it makes total spiritual sense.

The horrors of the inquisition were created by the ignorance & the greed of Men; it had absolutely nothing to do with Jesus' loving message. What the Witches believe in the past and in the present aligned perfectly with my beloved Master Jesus's message. My alignment became even stronger connecting with a past life. I knew there and then that one of my purposes in life was to be the bridge between Magic & Logic (Right & Left sides of the brain) to:

Show similarities where people see differences,
Expand the possibilities when people feel limited,
Show collaboration when people sense competition, and
Boost self-awareness and self-esteem worldwide.

Later when I become a Business & Life Coach, I learned the power of using archetypes with people and companies. Archetypes are everywhere, but most people have no idea of their power and how to use them. Successful companies use them all the time. So I decided to use this powerful strategy for my partnership plan as a tool to identify and understand our inner tendencies and those of our partners.

"Sex pleasures the body.

Love pleasures the heart.

Having both is sublime."

"Everything is dual"

Kybalion

THE POLARITY

Check the list of 12 archetypes on page 75. Ask yourself:

If you had to pick just one, which archetype best represents you?

Are you represented by the same archetype in different sides of your life (Family, Friends, Love, Work, etc)?

Which is your strongest personal archetype?
Which archetype best represents your last partner?
Which archetype best represents your best past partner?
Which archetype best represents your ideal partner?

Based on the main characteristics of the archetypes chosen above, do you think your personal archetype and your ideal partner's archetype are a good match? Why?

Does your personal archetype prevent you from or propel you towards materializing your ideal partner?

Is your personal archetype behaving like an "arch hero" or an "arch villain" toward your goal of materializing your ideal partner?

Are the archetypes you have been dating the type you desire? If not, why do you think that is?

What can you do to attract more of your ideal partner's archetype?

When you attract your ideal archetype, do you think the two of you will be a good match for each other? Why?

137

Happily moved on my workshop tour in Europe
Austria, Germany, Portugal & UK

**Life has its rhythm and moves.
I have my rhythm and style.
Shall we dance?**

THE STAGNATION

One of my male friends has been single for a very long time: no partner whatsoever for about 10 years. No hugs, no kisses, no sex, nothing: a real celibacy! Ouch! Can you believe it? He totally trapped himself three times in an undesirable life of celibacy. In my opinion, he is one of those people who like to suffer, fooling themselves that they are doing it for the good of others, when in fact is out of fear to face and live a full life. People like that get "comfortable" in uncomfortable situations. Instead of doing something about it, they just play victims or martyrs of the situations. Three times in his life he spent years wasting his life coping with problems that only existed in his mind, because of fear or laziness to check the possibilities and to enhance his reality. He created his own "Hell", but he kept saying that he was OK with the "heat". What a waste of a good life!

The first undesired celibacy started during a regular check up, when the doctor misdiagnosed him as being HIV positive. He was devastated with the diagnosis, but he never told anyone, and he never even considered to have a second opinion or a second test. In his mind, he played "the martyr" role and shut down from the possibility of having any emotional or sexual relationship, because he didn't want to risk infecting anyone. For many years he kept his celibacy and his secret all alone, until one day he had to do another check up for work, and this time he found out that he was not HIV positive. He could not believe his luck. He finally had no more excuses and found a girlfriend.

His girlfriend had herpes and they had unprotected sex, so when they broke up he automatically assumed he had herpes, and the second undesired celibacy started. He never went to the doctor to check and he never told anyone: not his parents, not his best friend, nobody. Once again, he got comfortable playing the "martyr" and remained celibate for many years. During the course of his second "martyrdom" he met me and we became friends.

Five years into our friendship, we were coming back from the movies, and my friend turned to tell me the biggest secrets of his life. He said he never ever told anyone, but as he considered me his best friend, he wanted me to know. Until that moment I had no clue what he was talking about, but I was already very touched and honored by his trust. Once he told me about the HIV & herpes stories and how those situations prevented him from dating anyone for 10 years, I was overwhelmed! WOW! I suddenly got very emotional and I could not help my tears coming down with a mix of gratitude for his trust and sadness his self-imposed punishment. I told him that I knew people who had herpes and HIV that lived a full happy life with their partners, kids and the whole nine yards. They were open with their partners about their diseases and they learned how to handle the situation. I told him he didn't have to give up anything because of his situation.

As naive as anyone can be, I asked why he shared his secret with me instead of with his best friend whom he had known for ages and with whom he hung out every single weekend. This conversation happened while I was driving and as I could not find a spot to park the car, in shock over his revelation I kept driving. I finally found a place to stop to give him my full attention. Suddenly he placed his hand over mine and said:
"You know why I trust you. Don't you?"
"No!" I said.
"Because I love you!"

Without any hesitation I instantly replied:
"That's so sweet! I love you too and treasure your trust!"
While holding my hand he continued:
"So let's take it to the next level!"
"WHAT???"
"MariLiza, I've loved you since the very first time I laid my eyes on you over 5 years ago. You are everything I ever wanted in a woman. You are beautiful, intelligent, honest, brave, successful, compassionate, and so much more. I think we will be great together."
"What are you talking about? I love you as a friend, just like a brother. I never saw this coming! I am honored with your love, but I am not attracted to you in that way. Have I ever given you any indication to the contrary?"

He was embarrassed, but kept trying to reason me into believing that we had everything going for us:
"No! You never said or did anything to mislead me, but I just hoped for so many years that one day we could be more than just friends."
As if someone hit me over the head, it was clear that he was not sharing his secrets with me because he was my friend; it was because he wanted to be more than just friends. I tried my best to be grateful for his affection but also to be clear that there was no way we would ever be together as a couple.

As his friend I wanted him to live a full happy life, and I kept asking about his health conditions and what he could do to enjoy life fully. After many vague answers, he finally told me that he never even went to the doctor to be tested for herpes. WHAT? I was in total disbelief! He just assumed that he had herpes, because he had unsafe sex with his ex girlfriend. In his mind he had herpes as well. I was shocked with his "loser" behavior. How could he just assume and not even try anything?

"Come on! You must go to a doctor and be tested. If you really have herpes, then you have to find out what type of herpes and how to live a full life."

It took many conversations over many years to convince him to finally to check it. Can you believe it? Oh My Great Goddess, what a waste of life. Unbelievable! Finally he went to the doctor and guess what? He didn't have herpes at all! The second amazing blessing in his life! I couldn't believe how many years he spent in unnecessary celibacy out of laziness, cowardice or both. All that waste of time, life and love made me nauseous.

Time went by, I kept dating other guys, hoping that my friend would finally live a full life and meet someone. Many years later, I met someone that I was falling in love with, and I wanted my friend to meet him. To my complete surprise my friend refused.

"Why not?" I asked him very upset and confused.

"MariLiza, I still love you and I will forever love you. What you are asking me is too hard. I wish you the best, but I just don't want to see it."

As if hit by a hammer, I realized that all those years I had become his third "imaginary disease" and he trapped himself in his third undesired celibacy. Oh no! I made sure he understood once and for all that he should move on, as we would never be a couple, even if I was single and alone. I loved him as a friend only. It was really tough to see that he only wanted to be in my life if things were going bad, but not when they were going well. I said:

"So when I marry someone, you won't be at my wedding? When I have kids, you won't come to visit me? What type of friendship is that?" I was so damn upset with all this waste of time, love and life. I'd never accept to be anyone's excuse to stop living.

It took ages for him to understand that we can have many loves in our hearts. We don't have to stop loving someone to love someone else. Actually I think once we truly love someone, they stay in our hearts forever. Thank GODDESS our heart can be infinitely big to love as many people as we want. Throughout the years I have tried to help him find someone he likes, but he always refused.

When I asked him to describe his ideal partner, he would say: *"I want a nice girl!"*
For which I replied: "Define nice girl!"
"I want a beautiful girl!"
"What do you consider a beautiful girl?"
"I want an intelligent girl!
With a smirk I said: *"How do you measure intelligence?"*
"MariLiza, you complicate things. I am OK with my life. I am not complaining or anything."
"But if you can't describe your ideal partner, how can you recognize her if she pass by you?", I said.
"Well, I have to be friends with her first for a few years to know who she really is than I can date her."
"You must be kidding! Right? Do you expect a woman to be your friend for years so one day you can figure out if she fits into your vague ideal partner? Do you believe after approaching her, she will magically be interested in becoming more than friends? Do you think this is an effective approach?"
And waiving his hand as if I was a little bee buzzing in his ears, he said: *"Leave it as it is. I am OK with my life."*

I *know*! It's hard to believe that some people choose to be trapped in an unhealthy rhythm. I had enough! Case closed! I was happy that thanks to my extreme persistence as a friend he went to the doctor and found out he was disease free. I just hoped he wouldn't find something or someone else as an excuse not to live.

"Everything flows, out and in;
everything has its tides"

Kybalion

THE RHYTHM

What effective and ineffective patterns do you see in your Partners Timeline?

In what rhythm do those patterns tend to come about?

Which beliefs or behaviors can you implement to change your patterns and rhythm and get closer to your desired partnership?

When and how are you going to implement those beliefs and behaviors?

Grateful at the Lotus temple
The Baha'i House of Worship
New Delhi, India

**Counting my blessings daily
&
finding more daily blessings!**

THE GRATITUDE

I've always considered myself optimistic and grateful. My natural inclination was to look on the bright side of things, and because of that my natural tendency was to be grateful for the gifts along the way. My parents were hard workers with two jobs each, to support three children and pay for all our education from primary school all the way to University. They did an amazing job as providers, role models and loving parents. The opportunity they were giving to us, they never had themselves.

My Dad Pedro worked since he was 11 years young and he only had the opportunity to finish primary school before getting married at 21 years young. My Mom Maria had a better opportunity and finished high school before getting married at 18 years young. They both worked very hard. My Dad became a ship supervisor at the Port and my Mom became a teacher in two schools. My Dad used to take Mom on his push bike when she was pregnant (expecting me) and take her all the way up to a mountain in a poor neighborhood where she would teach all day and many nights. Even when I was already born, they continued work hard, but I never ever heard them complaining about anything; instead they laughed and we enjoyed our simple life as much as we could. They were grateful for everything in their life even the simple and usual things; like a sunny day.

From my parents I've learned the MAGICAL ingredient to materialize anything in life: to be truly thankful. Being "truly thankful" and being "full of thanks" are two completely different things. I noticed I had some friends that were full of thanks, but even at an early age I could sense it was a kind of "automatic answer"; they didn't really mean it. Even though they pronounced the word "Thanks" it was empty of gratitude. It was just a word, not an expression of true gratitude.

When we are "FULL OF THANKS", we just say "Thank You" and say it automatically from our mind.

When we are "TRULY THANKFUL", we really mean "Thank You"and say it with gratitude from our heart.

The more I traveled, studied, and lived, the more I witnessed magical "gifts" everywhere, but people easily dismiss them by calling "coincidences". As many people consider themselves too busy to notice daily "magical" moments, they gradually lose their sense of "AWE" for life.

Just like an unused muscle, their sense of wonder atrophies. We take so much for granted daily that every day less and less we notice the blessing surrounding us that we atrophy our "power" to attract "luck". If we focus on all the things we don't have, we start operating in "poverty mode" and we will bring less and less into our life. This also applies for relationships.

"ATTRACTIVE

=

HAPPY + ACTIVE"

"Every cause has its effect;
every effect has its cause"

Kybalion

THE CAUSE & EFFECT

The trickiest part of my partnership plan is to explain this essential secret ingredient. It's a direct result of having created your vision, mission and values and living with gratitude. For some people it's easy to understand, but for others, not so much. I only managed to materialize my ideal partner when I did my part, and also when I didn't count on or depend on it to live happy every day. It's when you wish for something, but you don't need it to be fulfilled in order for you to be happy. Ask with detachment.

THANK with real GRATITUDE
for loving all you already have.

ASK with true DETACHMENT
for being already happy with your life.

AIM with higher intentions for the GOOD OF ALL
moving from the "I" mode to the "WE" mode

Have you ever thanked, at least in your mind, your ex-partners for their contribution in your journey? Why not? If you focus on the goodness that every experience can bring in your life, you will expand your power to transform your life and each time bring a better partner into your life.

At first it can be challenging to thank someone — even just in our mind — who has broken our heart in the past, but if you focus on the important lessons that experience brought you, your transformation will be incredible.

GRATITUDE EXERCISE

Make this exercise part of your daily health routine, and after a while you will see amazing differences. Not only say thanks for your blessings, but also for the blessings of people and partners along the way.

Every day, choose 2 different things to be thankful for, and also choose one ex-partner or person in your mind and thank him/her for something you received or learned. This exercise is simple, yet very powerful.

"I'm truly blessed for

having ____ (what),

because ____ (why).

I am so happy and

grateful for ____ (what),

because ____ (why?).

With all my heart,

THANK YOU for ____ (who),

because ____ (why)."

Having a ball in Bollywood with
my masculine & feminine energies!
Mumbai, India.

The power of embracing life's Yin & Yang!

THE ATTRACTION

I have been always totally supportive toward freedom of
sexual orientation, gay marriage, sex change or whatever
people want to express love for themselves and others.
I always thought homosexuality was natural. In my
heart there is acceptance for homosexual, heterosexual,
bisexual, trans gender and any other form of sexual
orientation. In my life I've always been heterosexual. I had
only eyes and desire for Men; especially the good looking
ones! My sexual orientation was never questioned or
shaken until my first trip to India.

As I was an experienced backpacker and traveled around
the world many times for long periods of time, I loved the
challenges and the thrill of doing what I love on my own.
On this trip I was traveling for almost one year through
13 countries, mostly in South East Asia. What an amazing
part of the world! On my first day in Mumbai, I walked
around with my backpack to find a clean and cheap place
to stay. As I never book places in advance, the first day is
always a challenge, but it allowed me to be more flexible
to change my itinerary any way I wanted. There was no
youth hostel in Mumbay and the accommodation I found
was dirty and pricey by Indian standards. While waiting
to talk about availability in this other place, I heard the
couple in front of me being told that the place was full
and there were no more places available. Oh! Oh! I was
hungry, tired of carrying my heavy backpack and it was
getting dark. As a woman alone in a new place it's not a
good idea to venture aimlessly at night. I could not help
but hear the couple taking about another option nearby, so
I followed them without their knowledge. The pursuit took
me to a dorm space at the Salvation Army. WOW! Can you
believe it? I never knew the Salvation Army had dorms.

It was a weird funny feeling to be there. The place was under construction and apart from the "not so clean place", there was construction mess as well. I had no option, it was too late at night to wander around, and I was exhausted. I got an upper bunk bed in a women's dorm with 12 other ladies. As soon as I arrived I met the lady staying on the lower part of my bunk bed. We clicked immediately as if we had known each other for ages. From that moment we were together 24/7 for the next 2 weeks. I was finishing my one year round the world trip in India, and she was starting her month-long trip in India.

After our first conversation, she invited me for dinner and a fun experience next day as extras in a Bollywood movie in Mumbai. After hours of driving in a van with a bunch of clueless foreigners like us and 2 Indian guys who spoke very broken English, we finally arrived at the movie set.

Forget any glamour of Hollywood; this was a low budget Bollywood movie. The plot was hilarious for me, because we — the bunch of foreigners — were pretending to be British cops (Bobbies), and my friend was British and I lived in the UK before for many years. We had a ball and kept having fun in all the cities we visited together until we reached the beautiful Palolem beach in Goa. I really needed to stay in just one place and relax for a week before going back to New York.

Most people don't realize that on long around the world trips, backpackers need a vacation within a vacation. I know it sounds weird for most people, but when you travel for months on end as backpackers, there are no luxuries. We want to extend our experience for as long as possible, instead of spending money in luxury hotels. Every day we have to figure out everything: places to visit, places to eat, how to get there, find train/bus/subway schedules, get to and from airports, meet new people every day, be amazed & cope with all sorts of emotions while traveling, every day, over and over again. It becomes a job to be a tourist and it drains you mentally, physically, financially, and emotionally. Many backpackers like myself stay months traveling alone, so we go through loneliness, sickness, depression and anxiety, as well as excitement, freedom, curiosity and all sorts of feelings, but all those feelings with no one to share them with. Nobody knows you and you don't know anyone for many months. It's tough in a way but in my opinion super worth it as it builds character. We learn how to rely on ourselves and make the best of all situations, no matter how good or bad.

I was exhausted emotionally, but extremely happy with my year off traveling around the world. Wohooo! I was proud to have visited 13 countries, mostly in Southeast Asia and India was my last stop. My new British friend and I got along super well, and we felt comfortable to share a lot of good and bad times of our lives with each other while sunbathing on the beach. I needed this relaxing time for different reasons than her, and we met at amazing turning points of our lives.

After almost 10 days together 24 hours a day sharing everything - accommodation, food, transportation, entertainment - we were super comfortable with each other as if we'd been friend forever. One day I woke up screaming from a weird dream where I was having an affair with my new friend. What? Me dreaming about having sex with a woman? WOW! I was too embarrassed to tell my friend about it, when she asked from the next bed what was going on. For the next few days I felt a certain attraction towards her. Weird! What is going on here? I never had those weird feelings toward a woman in my whole life. Am I becoming gay, or am I just emotionally confused for being so long alone? What is this? In all fairness to my heterosexual ego, it only happened a few moments, that weird attraction. Of course, I was traveling for too long without dating anyone, so it could be hormonal too.

This was really just a brief moment of attraction, but from that experience what really mattered to me was to understand more than ever before how hard it must be for people to confront unusual feelings towards the same sex. Unfortunately, many cultures still discriminate against it. I remembered when I was having that glimpse of attraction for another woman that my first thought was: "What would my Mom & Dad say? Would they be ashamed of me?" As Brazilian culture is unfortunately still too "macho" oriented and has a long way to go to accept and respect homosexuality. I realized that my fear was not about accepting myself as straight or gay; my fear was to disappoint the ones I loved. That very brief moment of unexpected attraction gave me an even deeper dimension of compassion and understanding for my beloved gay friends. Those few moments of attraction served a greater purpose in my life, to see that we all — men & women — have inside us feminine & masculine energy.

We all have Yin & Yang energies. They are both good and they both bring amazing qualities to our lives. When humans accept and respect this natural fact, this world will be a much better place. I realized that every partnership brings those energies to play, but it does not have to be 100% feminine energy from Women and 100% masculine energy from Men. In fact, those energies can be a mixture from each partner. What is important for a healthy relationship is that we have those energies balanced and in harmony. I looked deeper into my energy center and made sure, from that point on, to let both feminine (Yin) and masculine (Yang) energies play in harmony, regardless of my sex or my sexual orientation.

Unfortunately, I have seen women dismissing good men just because they were too "soft", and men dismissing great women because they were too "strong". Often enough, people have such rigid "scripts" of what a woman is supposed to be and what a man is supposed to be, that there is no room for authenticity. Based on their communities or society standards, they dismiss their feeling for the partner because they are too afraid to confront what family and society will say. Our dual energy is natural and divine, the more we let them flow in harmony, the more compassionate we become and the happier we get.

"Accepting our inner duality

is divine.

Letting them flow free

is sublime."

"Gender is in everything"

Kybalion

THE GENDER

Have you ever dismissed a partner or prospective partner just because he/she did not fit into the stereotypical description of a Man or a Woman in terms of appearance and behavior?

Who has been influencing your choices in partners? Religion? Family? Friends? Other?

Regardless of your gender or sexual preference, what is the type of energy more present in your life: Yin or Yang?

Is your predominant energy flowing naturally or are you forcing it to conform to what is expected of you?

Do you believe it's OK to have both Yin & Yang (feminine & masculine) energies in your life?

Do you allow the Yin & Yang energies to flow naturally in your life?

What happens when you allow Yin & Yang to flow naturally in your life?

What can you do to balance the Yin & Yang in your life?

Making dreams come true,
one year traveling alone through 13 countries.

*"Reality is reflected by our thoughts, propagated
by our words and manifested by our actions.*

MariLiza

THE ATTITUDE

As a business coach, one of the important things I've learnt is to model excellence by finding and applying successful strategies. If I want to be more successful in anything I have to attune my beliefs and behavior. One way to do that is to model known strategies from role models of the success we want. It doesn't matter what the goal is, nor who is the role model; what really matters is to choose an effective attitude toward the goal. In general we can choose to be reactive or proactive.

Reflecting on that reminded me of two famous Disney leading ladies: *Sleeping Beauty* & *Cinderella*. Sleeping Beauty took the reactive role, dreaming and waiting to be rescued by the prince to live a happy life. Cinderella, despite her rough environment, took the proactive role creating moments of joy in her daily life and taking risks to live the life of her dreams.

I suddenly realized that I have been very proactive in almost every single aspect of my life: happiness, health, family, friends, career, traveling, spirituality, education, dancing, finances, etc. However there was one important part missing: my love life. It took me by surprise to realize that I'd been reactive in this department. I was waiting to be "found" by the right partner to share my life. It's funny how I suddenly saw myself as a Sleeping Beauty waiting for my prince to find me, fight all the battles alone to reach me and finally make the move. *"WOW! MariLiza wake up! It's time to enjoy the proactive party!"*

That is when I decided to create my partnership plan, inspired by my knowledge from Wall Street about business plans.

Here I went from "I.T. girl" to become the "*IT* LADY"!
Wohoo! I gathered all my knowledge from my magical
side (right brain) and from my logical side (left brain) to
be fully invested in my partnership plan. I created daily,
weekly, monthly, and quarterly commitments to invest
time, money and efforts to materialize my ideal partner.

Because I believe in GODDESS' universal laws and bigger
plan, of course, I acknowledged the possibility that finding
my ideal partners might not be in the "Divine cards" for
me in this life, but I was going to:

• live happy every day in a state of gratitude,
• give my best shot at materializing my ideal partner, and
• enjoy the process by detaching from the destination and
   focusing on the journey.

I made a short list to remind myself of my new role as
proactive partner to materialize my ideal love partner.

When REACTIVE	When PROACTIVE
I have a vague goal	I have a specific goal
I procrastinate	I have initiative
I compare myself with others	I collaborate with others
I have no responsibility	I am responsible
I blame others	I blame myself
I'm influenced by others	I'm influenced by my goal
I'm a passenger of life	I'm the driver of my life
I use one side of my brain	I use both sides of my brain
I do what is convenient	I do what is necessary
I'm Sleeping Beauty	I'm Awake Beauty

It was time to put the ACTIONS AT PLAY to:

- **DESIGN**

My action plan with daily, weekly, and monthly activities.
- **DEVELOP**

My belief and behaviors that support my self-love, joy and gratitude.
- **DELIVER**

Joy and Gratitude every day, as if I already have my ideal partner and everything I want towards accomplishing my mission in life.

**What approach are you
choosing to find, attract and
keep your Ideal Partner?**

THE PROACTIVITY

Plan your life based on your desired vision, mission, values and goals, and according to your priorities in life, add time and space to include steps to manifest your ideal partner in your schedule:

DAILY VISUALIZATIONS
      SAY   PROCLAMATIONS
      SEE   BLESSINGS
      SENSE MATERIALIZATION

WEEKLY TRANSFORMATIONS
      New BELIEFS
      New BEHAVIOR
      New BENEFITS
      New BELIEFS + New BEHAVIOR = New BENEFITS

MONTHLY MATERIALIZATIONS
      SCORE your SATISFACTION
      BALANCE PROS & CONS
      CHECK SCORE + BALANCE PROS & CONS = IMPROVEMENT

QUARTERLY INTERACTIONS
      PARTNER TEST DRIVE
      TWEAK OR THROW? LET IT BE OR LET IT GO?

YEARLY EVALUATIONS
      HEALTHY PARTNERSHIPS
      PARTNERSHIP PLAN

Check the purpose of your life by connecting with your higher self or spiritual connection.

Finding new ways to enjoy the journey.
Great Ocean Road, AUSTRALIA.

**Learning to say Bye
before saying Hi!**

THE START & END

After recovering from a deep depression caused by the end of my first marriage, all I wanted was to travel, have fun and no strings attached. A friend invited me to go to Mexico for a week and off we went for the most wanted duo: sun & fun. Wohoo!

My self-esteem was back into shape and I was feeling damn good, when we entered the famous *Señor Frog* in Cancun. My skin was chocolate tanned and my sexy yellow top made it boost even more.

As usual I didn't drink anything, and yet many people would think I had a few drinks. To have fun has always been very easy for me. It was never about the place but about my choice of attitude & company. I couldn't be happier, as I was doing what I love (traveling) with someone I love (my friend).

People who don't know me are always surprised to discover that I can dance and party all night and never taste an alcoholic drink. Throughout my life I had tasted the usual drinks: wine, beer, whiskey, rum, liquor, but nothing appealed to my taste buds. I don't even like sodas, coffee or packaged juices. My favorite drinks are tea, milk, and especially fresh squeezed fruit juices - Mmmmm!

But going back to the real juicy stuff – The Men – my friend and I were sitting at the table enjoying our dinner while looking at the people chatting, dancing, and flirting around us. Mmmmm! There were so many good-looking manly dishes to choose from. Ai! Ai! Ai! Suddenly out of nowhere, a "Greek God" materialized in front of our table, smiling at us with enchanting green eyes:

"Ladies, would you like to dance with me?"

My friend and I looked at each other in complete disbelief. We were impressed, attracted and very puzzled! He impressed us by his courage to come from nowhere and talk to us. In general, men don't like to be rejected so they take their time to first flirt from a distance to get some kind of signal of acceptance and then approach.

None of us had seen him or flirted with him, and yet there he was smiling and waiting for our answer. We were attracted – damn yeah – he was tall, and great looking. He could easily sweep any girl off her feet in any place. Last but definitely not least, we were completely puzzled by one single letter in his invitation: the "S". He said " LadieS, would you like to dance with me?" We were not sure if he was a true gentleman or a true player. That mystery spiced up our night.

We invited him to sit and join us for dinner, and once we were finished with dinner, we could dance with him. He said he would let us finish our dinner in peace and wait for us at the bar. Before he left I could not resist and asked: "Are you really brave or did you have a few drinks to come up here to invite us to dance?"

With humble eyes, he said: "I had to get a drink to boost my courage to talk to the most beautiful girls in Cancun." And with a gorgeous smile he left us in complete *Awe*! Oh My GG! *"What just happened?"*, we asked each other.

The night was starting in the best way possible. Wohoo! We did not know for sure who he was interested in, but it didn't matter because he made us feel good with the prospect of a fun night. I was not sure what was going to happen, but I was sure this was going to be a memorable night. We finished our dinner excited and we went straight to meet our Greek God, who was talking to few guys. After the proper introductions, we found out that they were friends traveling together, just like me and my girlfriend.

As soon as we hit the dance floor we could see clearly who he was aiming for and I confess I was thrilled. Wohooo! From the very start my friend and I realized that we were the "City Girls" and they were the "Country Boys". The Greek God turned out to be an American Hero – a firefighter from Indiana. Even though he had a bold move coming to talk to us, it was clear that he was shy, respectful, and excited to be dancing with me.

We danced all night and he treated me like a Lady, just the way I like it. His friends were dancing with my friends and they kept bringing drinks to us all the time. He was very surprised when I said I didn't drink any alcohol. He on the other hand was drinking a lot. I was not sure if it was because he was nervous or because he could not refuse his friends pushing drinks on him. He was getting drunk but he was still sweet and respectful.

After that day, the fireman and his friends called us to go out again. And once again we had a great time. We went out as a group a few times and he was always very protective and clearly interested but he didn't make any move until on our 4th date. My naughty self invited him to play a game and whoever won was granted a wish. His wish was granted: a magical kiss! Wohooo!

The next night he invited me to go for a walk alone with him on the beach in front of our hotel. The night was beautiful! Since the very first day, I trusted him. Not sure if it was my naiveté, or my intuition, but I felt safe with him. That would be our last night together before he head back to Indiana and me back to New York. We talked for a long time about our lives and we found out that we both just survived horrible divorces. We were both wounded and careful not to jump into anything. We were aware of our "rebound" phase and our desire for something light and refreshing. Five wonderful days feeling like teenagers were perfect with a sense of promising future opening up ahead of us.

Once again, he made a bold move and said: "I wish I could spend our last night together laying down and holding you in my arms until the sunrise." It was already 3 AM and he had to go back to his hotel to leave in the morning and catch his flight. I asked intrigued: *What are you suggesting?"*

With loving eyes he said: *"My wish is to kiss and hold you in my arms until we fall sleep for a few hours. I want to wake up next to you to see the sunrise. I promise I will respect you & your wishes."*
How could I resist those loving green eyes? I heard myself saying: *"That's so romantic! It may be completely crazy, but I trust you!"*
His big smile brightened even more on this unforgettable night.

We were both sharing rooms with our friends, so we called to assure them we were coming back in time for our flights, but only in the morning. He booked another room in my hotel so I could be close to my friends when he had to leave. My hotel was very expensive and I knew he was a hard working fireman so I really appreciated his efforts to give me the best accommodation, even though it was for just 5 hours. We were both a little shy when we entered the hotel room.

"You have no idea how hard it is for a man to resist your charms, but I really treasure your trust and I would never do anything to jeopardize it. Thanks for granting my wish, my beautiful Witch. You made me so happy!" He gave me a tender kiss, held me softly like the most precious gift and we both fell into a sweet dream for a few hours before leaving Cancun!

Once we returned to our different states in USA, he called me and invited me to visit him in Indiana and paid for the ticket and hotel. When I arrived to visit him 2 months after we met, he was so happy to see me that it melted my heart. He lived alone in his house but he rented a room for me in the best hotel in his city so I could feel more comfortable. When he helped me to my room, I asked him: *"Where are you going to sleep?"*

"Of course, I would love to be with you all the time, but you will be the one to decide when and where to grant my wish!"

"WOW! I was really impressed! This handsome hard working fireman was melting my heart big time."

After that we kept seeing each other every 2 months. Sometimes he came to visit me in New York, sometimes I went to visit him in Indiana. I met his adorable family and he wanted me to meet his daughter which he raised alone, sharing the custody with his ex-wife. Two years passed by in our relationship. He already declared his love, and he was inviting me to move in or to move nearby. He said he could never leave his city because of the love for his daughter, family and job.
It was then that I had one of my proudest moments in a relationship. For the first time in my life, I put my feelings aside and looked in the future to see how my life would be

if I accepted to move into his life. I did a complete rational evaluation about our different lifestyles and goals in life. So I did a list of things I thought it were important to consider.

MY PERSONA	MY PARTNER
City girl	Country boy
Wants to live in different places	Wants to live in one place
Travels to different countries every year	Travels to the same place every year
Speaks 3 languages and wants to learn more	Speaks one language and does not want to learn more
Brazilian	American
Portuguese	English
Christian Witch	Roman Catholic
No kids, but wants to have kids	One kid, doesn't want more kids

The list of differences could go on longer, but I realized that for this relationship to really exist I was the only one who would have to be flexible and give up everything.

I would have to give up: job, friends, lifestyle and dreams and he could not and would not do the same for me ever. He could not do the same for me, not because he was bad or mean. No! Not at all! It was just not in his nature. It's like asking a dog to fly. And I was considering to stop flying to just walk. For the first time I realized I had to end this relationship because we wanted different things in life. Of course, I was a little sad to face the fact but I was happy with my maturity in seeing things for what they were and not for what I wanted them to be. I realized that as much as this relationship had given both of us a lot of joy, it was time to move on and leave it on a high note. I was very grateful to GODDESS for having allowed us to meet each other and care for each other. I just hoped in my heart that we could keep being friends after I broke up with him. As we lived so far away from each other and I did not want him to spend money and reschedule his job, daughter and life to see me just for me to break up with him, I decided to call.

As magical as the begging, so was the ending. I was afraid that he would be too hurt and never want to talk to me again when I explained to him all the reasons why I thought in the long run our relationship would not work. Even though if was my choice, I was crying on the phone when I was talking to him. He listened to everything and said: *"MariLiza, you are right! I totally agree with you, but I would never have the guts to break up with you. You are right! I can not give you what you want, and you totally deserve to get everything you want."*

I was so delighted with what I was hearing. I was breaking up with him and he was still supporting me with so much love and care. Oh My Great GODDESS! Thank you so much for helping both of us to come such a long and beautiful way!

That is one of my proudest moments. I had learned to look into the future, to stand up for my dreams and to be completely honest with my partner. And to my joy he was in the same stage of love and maturity. That was a very happy ending!

With this amazing episode I had learned that relationships, just like people, change and we should never expect to count on them forever. From now, instead of hoping for "Forever", I would take the "For as long as it lasts".
At my first wedding, bride & groom exchanged the usual vows "Till death do us part", but we did not fulfill our promise, so I promised myself to never promise things that I can not deliver.

From now on I would vow:

**"May this partnership last for as
long as love and respect remain."**

And so I did many years later when I married my beloved Vikingtastic partner.

Not considering the end of a relationship is like not considering that one day we are going to die. This is not a pessimistic approach at all; it's a way to prepare for the inevitable and be appreciative for the precious time we have left. We must consider the possibilities of a good end before it even starts, to make sure we value the journey and don't take the destination for granted. Great beginnings start with good endings.

"When you know how to end,

you are ready to start."

**Do you know how to appreciate
the start & the end??**

THE EXTREMES

You must be thinking:

"What does this story of a relationship ending well have to do with materializing my ideal partner?"

My answer is: EVERYTHING!

When we know and understand all the phases of a relationship, we can move through them more freely and gracefully. When we understand that relationships have cycles, we learn how to deal with the high and low tides on the emotional sea of relationships.

In general, people see the growing wave a of new relationship as exciting & desirable, and the crashing of the wave of the relationship as scary & devastating. But if we expand this limiting perspective by understanding that the cycle of the waves is natural and we have the choice of how and when to "surf" that wave, we bring awareness to the nature of relationships and take responsibility for practicing to be a better surfer every day.

Great surfers enjoy every step of the journey; not only when they are on top of the wave. The great surfers of life spend most of their time working to reach the right spot, waiting for the right wave, and then starting all over again. All those hours of hard work to try to be on top of the wave for a few moments. For most of us, non-surfers, that sounds crazy, but if you think about all the successful people in many different fields — love, business, arts, science, etc — we notice that they have learnt to perform well and love each step of the way.

Enjoy your ride on the roller coaster of partnerships!

So that partnership with a great beginning & a great ending with the fireman was a wonderful achievement to me. I managed, for the first time in my life, to be mindful toward myself and toward my partner from start to end. And when you end a partnership well, it's not over; it's just transformed. And in this case we went from loving partners to loving friends. The love and care for each other didn't finish, it just transformed. Thinking of that partnership always brings a smile to my face as something done well and preserved well by both parties.

Of course, we can not do both — sometimes we meet and interact with people who don't understand that everything changes and they can't accept and cope with the changes.

What relationships in your life — love, friendship, business, etc — had a good beginning & a good ending when the time of changes came?

What phases of a relationship can you improve?

How are you going to improve those phases?

"Embrace changes

to

change your life."

On my honeymoon with my Vikingtastic
Partner on a great safari.

Chitwan National Park, NEPAL

**Time & Resource management help
to make dreams come true.**

THE MANAGEMENT

One day I was studying time management and priorities, and I decided to make a list of the most important parts of my life. I listed: spirituality, family, friends, partner, health, travel, work, fun and a few other things. Then I checked what were my priorities and how much time and effort I spent with each part.

It was kind of a slap on my spirit to realize that even though spirituality was at the top of my list, I had no scheduled time for it at all. Sure, I prayed for three minutes every day before going to sleep, but if spirituality was so important as I showed on my list, then I was missing out on my commitment to what I valued most.

So since that day, I reserved a specific day of the week (Mondays), a specific time (11pm), and a specific length of time (45 min) to dedicate to my spiritual studies. I also committed with my spiritual guides to assist me, so my commitment was no longer just with myself, but also with my spiritual guides and spiritual guests who are invited to join me every week to expand Unconditional Love & Divine Light in our lives. It's been wonderful to keep this sacred moment no matter what happens in my life, no matter where I am in the world, and no matter who I am with.

For the last 10 years I am proud to say that I did not miss one day. It was a small, but very important step towards my spiritual enlightenment. Later I slowly added more commitments on my spiritual journey. The best things in life come from our commitment to keep doing the best we can on a consistent basis every step of the way, until we reach our goal, and then...we keep going even further.

183

The same principle applies to whatever we want to achieve in life: health, happiness, business, friendship, etc, and even to achieve an ideal partner. So if I wanted to have my ideal partner I also had to commit to a routine and give my best efforts consistently. That is when I started visualizing my ideal partner every day for 10 minutes first thing in the morning, with all the specific dimensions (Physical, Mental, Emotional, and Spiritual), details (Musts & Wants) and using all my six senses.

If nothing else, the vision of seeing me and my ideal partner — sitting on my bed, one in front of the other in a Lotus position, meditating together with our hands slightly touching each other — always made me smile happy and start the day grateful.

"Commit to a daily routine.

Give your best efforts

consistently."

What are the most important things in your life?

Are they scheduled as priorities in your life?

THE PRIORITIES

The key is not to prioritize what is in your agenda, but to schedule your priorities so that you can fit your agenda into the schedule of priorities.

STEPS TO ORGANIZE YOUR PRIORITIES

- **IDENTIFY YOUR ROLES**
Write down your key roles like: parent, spouse, friend, manager, athlete, volunteer, student, etc.
- **SELECT YOUR GOALS**
For each of your important roles, choose one goal *to be achieved within the next 7 days.*
- **SCHEDULE**
Now, with the information above you can plan your week accordingly and put them in a calendar on your computer, tablet and/or phone. Make it consistent between all your gadgets. Sunday is normally a good day to plan the week ahead.

The same way you would save time to spend with your ideal partner, you will save time with your commitment to materialize him/her. If you desired to be in touch with your ideal partner when he/she arrives in you life, then spend at least 10 minutes a day "talking" and visualizing him or her as if your ideal partner already exists in you life. You can talk to him/her about your life, you can thank him/her for doing something for you. I know it may sound a little out there, and that is good, because you want to reach him/her somewhere out there, and spending time with him/her will amplify your vibration on a regular basis. So check your priorities, choose your goals, and set your actions by putting first things first.

Celebrating Samhain.
New York, USA

FROM "ME & YOU" TO "US"

THE STORY

WAVE CYCLES

Choosing to pay attention not only to my partners timeline but especially to my life timeline, I noticed a clear pattern that I called the pulse of my life; the remarkable transformations that happen in my life every three to five years. What most people hate, I love: CHANGES! I never said I was normal, just happy!

So after 5 years working in Wall Street, living in New York City and being happily single, I was ready for some exciting change. My Dad used to call me: *"8 or 800"*. He used to say that I was everything or nothing: pure extremes. According to him I had no "80", meaning "no middle ground". Only much later in life I realized he was absolutely right! Time was flying by and I wanted to change everything at once: a new career, a new country and a new marital status! Oh! Yes! Who says we can not have it all?

GIPSY HEART

My passion for traveling took me to 60 countries so far. And I loved them all, but when people ask me what is my favorite, my answer is always the same one: "The next unknown country". My home had been Brazil, UK and USA, with many years spent in each, so I knew I could live happily anywhere. I was ready for a new home, a new job and a new man. Wohooo!

It was time to call Australia my next home. I had been to Australia a few times, and loved the country and the easy-going Aussies. For the first time in my life I was planning to move to a new country where I actually had a few friends living already.

As the immigration process in "Aussie land" was favorable to people with IT skills like Systems Analyst, in my mind I was half-way there already. It would take one year to complete the immigration process and get a working visa, but I was in no hurry.

As I knew I could live happily anywhere — been there, done it — I was totally open to the possibility of finding a partner anywhere around the world, so I thought to myself: "Why not add my profile to a good dating site in Australia? Who knows, maybe I could meet someone even before my arrival?" The idea sounded appealing for two reasons:

1 - It was a different approach – An "outside the box" idea which was as crucial part of my new partnership plan.
2 - I had nothing to lose and everything to gain.

MIND PROCESS (INFO GATHERING)

I talked to my Aussie friend whom I met in New York and who later moved back to Melbourne, Australia. He gave me the name of the biggest and best dating site in Australia. With that in mind, I gathered information about best practices of online dating from a Brazilian friend who was a "PRO" of online dating. She had it all from her online experience: she dated a lot, she got engaged a few times, and eventually she got married with a guy from a different country. She used online dating for years, from the old "ICQ" times all the way to the current online dating.

Packed with an Aussie tip on "where", and Brazilian tips on

"how", there I went onto my second attempt to internet dating in a totally new country.

OUT OF THE COMFORT ZONE

My preferred approach has always been the old-fashion courtship style where men take the first steps toward the women. Thank Goddess, I never had any problem in this department. Plenty of opportunities came my way with guys flirting with me and asking me out, but their quality & chemistry were not quite what I wanted. According to my partnership plan, I had to do things differently to get different results and evaluate the direction in which those results lead me. So I decided to get out of my comfort zone and be more proactive toward my ideal partner.

For the first time ever I decided to take the first step to contact potential partners. I used the search option in the dating site to find prospective partners among thousands of male profiles online.

One of my earlier "self-esteem" decisions was to no longer pay for any dating site. After all, the dating site was lucky enough to have the quality of my profile in their list. *They* should be paying *me* to be there. Ha! Ha! Ha! If we don't consider ourselves a great catch, who *will*?

After a few months on the dating site, I had a large quantity of replies, but small quality of answers, just like in the dating site in the USA; nothing special to raise my eyebrows. In general, men look at women's photos and if they consider the women attractive, hot, sexy, or beautiful, then they don't even bother reading the women's profiles to check if they are a good match and vice-versa. Nope! They just shoot blindly, foolishly, and cockily to as many as women as possible!

THE PROSPECTS

In my first attempt to make the "first move" and search and signal, I found someone interesting and good-looking. As a "non paying" member of the dating site, I was only allowed to post my profile and send virtual "kisses" for free, and I could only send e-mails if I bought credits for it, and that I already decided I was not going to do anymore. So the good-looking guy replied with a free virtual kiss back, as a hint for me to pay and contact him. I sent him a second free virtual kiss, implying that if he wanted to contact me he would have to make the effort to pay for it. Guess what? The guy sent his second free virtual kiss. In my opinion, there were two choices: either he was too slow to understand my hint, or he was too stingy to pay for it; either way this guy was not for me. Next!

A few weeks passed and I made another attempt to get out of my comfy zone and look for a good prospective partner. There were a few interesting prospects, so I sent my virtual kiss to the one I thought was the best. A day later he sent me a virtual kiss back. As I was set on my decision not to pay for contacting men anymore (to be a different approach from a previous experience in USA), I sent my second virtual kiss to send a message that I was interested in contacting him, but I was not interested in paying for it.

To my delightful surprise, he paid for the credits and wrote to me the next day with the best e-mail I have ever received from a man in my whole life. Wohooo! Believe me, by that time I was a "PRO" in reading not only between the lines, but also the lack of lines from the experience of receiving hundreds of e-mails from men throughout the years in USA. In my experience, 95% were

what I call "one liners"; the type of guys who introduce themselves like:
"Hey hottie, what's up?", *"You are F****** sexy, call me."*, *"Let's hook up tonight!"* and other "gems" of the English literature.

The other 5% were what I call the "one poster" guys who write a long essay about themselves (or about what they want you to believe they are) and send the same to every woman, regardless of what they say on their profile.

THE SURPRISE

So you can imagine my astonishment when I received this polite, intelligent, humble and very well written e-mail. Not only was he polite, humble, good-looking, and single, but also...he could read & write. OMGG! Not a small achievement in the age of "I c u" (instead of "I see you").

But "seeing someone" does not mean "getting someone". They are two very different things. Aren't they? Anyway, this prospective partner was looking better & better by the minutes and by the letters. I was not sure if this initial connection was going anywhere, but just the glimpse of the amazing possibilities ahead took my breath away on my way to find my amazing MAN (Yes! With capital letters all the way. ;-)

His e-mail excited me in many levels. He pleased my inner twins who have completely different tastes and styles. His name was ULF – "Wolf" in Swedish – which evoked Liza's wild fantasies. Meanwhile his intelligent e-mail was right up Mari's intellectual alley.

"What could a woman like you possibly have seen in a man like me?", He said with sincere humbleness.

"Have you looked in the mirror lately? Damn! You're great looking!", Liza replied. *"What a sweet humble man.",* Mari thought.

The more I read his kind compliments & intelligent questions, the more I could not believe how great this man seemed to be. But as I had learned to "hold my horses", which in my case is to "hold my twins", I breathed in and out to calm down my heart and hormones.

After holding back my initial explosion of excitement, and lowering my usual big expectations as much as possible, I sent a sweet and spicy reply. I thanked him for his kind words and for his effort in reaching out to me, and then I dropped my favorite "bomb" question, which scares the hell out of the average Joes: "What are your top 3 worst flaws?"

THE INVITATION

As I believe in being fair and honest, in my reply I also offered the opportunity for him to ask about my flaws. After all, the good stuff — our qualities — anyone can handle well, but the heavy stuff — our flaws — very few will be willing to try. As I like real (not virtual) connections, I mentioned my preference in talking (online or the phone) instead of sending e-mails back and forth. I answered all his smart questions and sent mine with an option to call me. To make things better, he preferred real-time connections, too. Wohoo!

As he was on the other side of the planet, our time difference was one of our challenges to talk. When I was awake, he was sleeping and vice-versa, but as one of my favorite quotes goes:

"When there's a will, there's a way."

THE BEST CALL EVER

A day later he called me, and it was the longest and best phone call I have ever had in my life. OMGG! It sounded too good to be true!

Can you guess how long we talked on the phone? Guess again! Higher! If you know me, you know that I love to talk, but I beat my own record of the longest non-stop conversation ever in my life. WE SPOKE 12 HOURS NON-STOP ON THE PHONE! Believe me, I was not the only one doing all the talking. He didn't sleep all night to talk to me, and I didn't eat all day to talk to him. Oh My Great GODDESS! Is it a great divine sign or what? Once again, I could see that my partnership plan was paying off with incredible possibilities. I was very proud of how I conducted the conversation: fun & frank. I had fun enjoying the moment teasing him, laughing with him, but I was also frank and straight to the point, asking the things that mattered the most to me, without any shame or hesitation.

The questions I asked him would have made any normal man run like crazy, and yet he replied to them as the most natural thing:

"*What are you looking for? Fun? Friendship? Love? Family?*"

"*Have you ever been married? Why not?*"

"*Do you have any kids? Do you want kids? Would you adopt kids?*"

"*When was your last relationship? How long did it last? Are you over it?*", and many other spicy questions that would

195

make the average Joes break into the sweat of their lives. Not only didn't Ulf shake or run, but he also answered all questions with ease. There was one or two questions that he did not have the answer for right away, so he asked if he could have a little bit of time to reflect upon them. His honesty and courtesy double impressed me.

The more we spoke on the phone, the more I was astonished with the quality of his character and the easiness of our conversation. "Ah! I loved his sexy voice too!", added excited Liza ;-)

THE SURPRISING COMMITMENT

After the first conversation we spoke every day for few hours. It was amazing how fast time flew talking to him. On the third day we talked on the phone, he said:
"I don't expect you to do the same, but I want you to know that I will delete my profile from the dating site, because from now on I just want to focus on knowing you and nobody else."

I could not believe how wonderful it was to hear this surprising commitment from him. In my experience, men never want to give up what they consider to be their freedom to look around and taste the possibilities for as long as possible.

"That's great! I feel the same way! I will delete mine too." The first conversation showed that we were looking for the same thing: a life partner. The second conversation displayed that we were both very interested to know each other. The third conversation marked the mutual commitment of following through.

My excitement was growing exponentially daily. Ai! Ai! Ai!

"When there's a will,

there's a way."

**How does the partnership
benefit each partner?**

THE BENEFITS

When analyzing my personal and professional life, I realized that in business my interactions were up-front and straight forward. However, in my personal life, not so much. I was digging deeper to find out how I could be more in my personal life like I was in my business life. While studying business, I've learned that there are 3 major types of interactions:

• LOSE/LOSE
Nobody intentionally chooses to be in this group. Normally what happens is that there are two stubborn individuals with ego-invested agendas interacting, so the result is that both lose. This is the classical behavior of enemies at war. Their motto would be something like:
"If nobody wins, then losing is not so bad."

• WIN/LOSE
In this interaction, there are two possibilities:

- I win, you lose
This is the "winning at any cost" approach. Here "Winning" is beating the adversary.

- I lose, you win
This is the "pleasing others at any cost" approach. Here "Winning" is pleasing the other.

• WIN/WIN
This interaction seeks mutual benefits. There is no competition, just cooperation. It's based on the belief that there is plenty for everybody. There is no need to achieve success at the expense or the exclusion of the other.

Those types of interactions not only apply to the business scenario, but also to human interactions — including the interaction with your ideal partner.

What quadrant best represents your past relationships?

What type of interactions did you have in your last relationship?

What type of interactions do you want?

What actions can you take to achieve your desired type of interaction?

When and how will you start those actions?

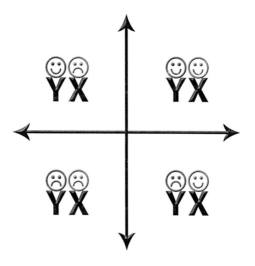

With the big astrologer.
Kuala Lumpur, Malaysia

Is our fate written in the stars?

THE MIND

Not sure where it comes from, but most of us — women in particular — have a tendency to want our partners to read our mind, so we don't have to ask for what we want; they just have to find out on their own. As crazy as it sounds, I still see men and women expecting mind reader partners. We assume we understand our partner, and also assume our partner understands us. Been there, and done it many times. It's not worth it.

I remember clearly one episode when I had a huge crush on a handsome guy in my English class. For almost two years I waited for him to "make a move". He was always flirting with me, dropping compliments then and there. A few times he invited me out for coffee after class and we always got along super well. Every time I saw him my heart beat excitedly with the possibility that this would be the day when he was going to make a move and be more than a friend. I fantasized about it so many times. Even though I had plenty of opportunities to ask the most important questions, I was too shy to ask and too proud to show signs that I was into him.

We both lived and worked in São Paulo city. I was from Santos — a beach town an hour away — and he had a beach condo not far from my family's house. One day a friend came to visit me from the UK, and I had the brilliant idea to show her the coast line from my parents' house to his beach condo. I had the perfect excuse to "be in the neighborhood" and stop by at his place to introduce my friend and practice English. I took my motorbike, she jumped on the back seat and off we went to check the beaches and the boys. In my case, I was looking forward to seeing one boy in particular.

When we got to his building, my heart was beating fast and my hands shaking with excitement. I was hoping he was there when I rang the bell of his apartment. To my delight he was there and said he would come down in 2 minutes. I was beside myself with joy as this opportunity turned out to work perfectly. He came down smiling showing off his tan and his big blue eyes. After the introductions, we started chatting at the door. Suddenly a woman come out of the building and walked straight in our direction. When he saw the woman he reached out toward her and introduced her to us: *"This is my girlfriend."*

Time and space froze after the bombastic word "girlfriend", or I froze, I don't know. I could not hear anything else. On the outside I was exchanging pleasantries, but on the inside I was shocked and devastated. I managed to "look normal" and made an excuse to leave saying that we came for a quick "Hi" as we were passing by. Every cell in my heart wanted to burst into tears. I had to leave immediately before my broken heart was exposed to the elements.

As soon as my friend and I were on my bike, I drove away in pain. I didn't know where to go, I just wanted to disappear from the face of the earth. After driving through a few streets like a zombie, I found a quiet place to park, and exploded into tears. My friend knew about my two-year crush on this guy, so she just sat on the sidewalk next to me and let me cry for a long time. This guy was the epiphany of everything I wanted in a partner: handsome, intelligent, gentleman, spoke two languages fluently, rich by his own merits, family oriented, and — until a few minutes ago — single.

I felt so stupid for never asking the most important question: "Do you have a girlfriend?"

I never asked and he never told me. I thought if he was in a relationship he would have told me. I was not sure what was hurting me more: the fact that he had a girlfriend, the fact that I waited for 2 years for his move, or the fact that I never dared to ask him the most important question.

It took me a while to stop crying and get back to my bike and on with my life, but I did and I promised to never ever again let myself fall into the "silence" trap. I wanted to be understood, but I never understood him. There and then I decided that from that moment on I would be up front and straight forward about my availability and inquire about the availability of others. I didn't want to waste my life waiting for illusions to come about.

**UNDERSTANDING BEFORE
BEING UNDERSTOOD**

THE COMMUNICATION

1. LOVE
The purpose of a partnership is simply to love & be loved.
No! It's to learn and grow. Growing together should be as important to love in your list.

2. DUTY
Your partner should be everything to you.
It's not anyone's job to be everything in someone's life. It sets up dependence and creates neediness on one side and resentment in the other.

3. PROPORTION
A partnership should be 50%-50%
Our partnerships are like a roller coaster; sometimes situations take the partnership up, and other times take it down. Be careful with keeping score! In general, people play this game because they are insecure. If you give to others from a place of self-respect and self-love it will be the right amount.

4. CONSISTENCY
You know your partner very well, so the partnership becomes predictable.
We are all creatures of change and variety. Of course, we are also creatures of habit. When we think we know our partner, we stop being present and aware of what is happening around us. Keep in mind that if we are always changing and doing unpredictable things, so are our partnerships.

5. ASSUMPTION
Your partner knows that you love him/her.
Watch out! It's easy to take a long relationship for granted.

6. FOREVER
You should love your partner no matter what.
Until we go to heaven, we live in an imperfect world with imperfect people who, sometimes, are not good for us. It's important to set boundaries and have standards. Love your partner, but first love yourself, because if you do, you will not allow any partner to continuously disrespect you.

7. TURBULENCE
If things get rough, it's best to cut your losses and leave.
Many people think that the grass is greener on the other side of the fence, and instead of working on the grass they'd rather jump the fence. However, they may soon realize that in the other side of the fence,the grass is also crappy. Partnerships can be like giving birth: painful, a lot of work, but hopefully the result makes everything worthwhile. What if our Mother said: "I had enough! I am out of here!"?

8. INTERDEPENDENCY
My partner should make me happy.
No! You should make yourself happy, and then share your happiness with your partner, and vice-versa. When we believe — because of naiveté or laziness — that it's someone's job to make us happy, we become reactive and resentful when we realize nobody is qualified for or interested in this job. Conquer your own independent happiness and share it with others, so when your partner shares his/her happiness with you, it creates a healthy interdependent partnership.

"We are born dependent,

we grow to be independent,

then

we strive to be interdependent."

Our first trip together in our first month together
Sydney, Australia

Are we both committed to building a partnership?

THE EFFECTS

One of the crucial parts of creating my partnership plan was to learn how evaluate the quality of the partnership based on its synergy. Synergy is the interaction or collaboration of two or more agents to produce a combined effect greater than the sum of their separate effects. The knowledge of when to avoid, when to improve and when to leave the partnership, is essential to build a healthy partnership.

In my life I could see clear relationship marks left along the way, but I wanted to learn especially how to see the "signs" before and during the partnership. I noticed that we tend to look at the overall "health" of our relationships only when it's sick or almost dead or buried. I realized it was crucial to have a periodical check up on the type of synergy created by the partnership in each phase of its life.

It's important to pay attention to the "side effects" of the partnership you are into or getting into. Check all the important areas of our lives: love, health, spirituality, personal development, friends, finances, etc. Once you analyze those "side effects" you can check the partnership "balance".

From my past partnerships, I noticed clear marks of decay along the way:

METAMORPHOSIS

When I was with my first boyfriend, I unconsciously distanced myself from all my male friends, because of his jealousy. When I was with my first husband, I felt like someone else. He was super talkative and loved to take all the spotlight all the time to himself, so unconsciously I had to keep my bubbly self aside and dimmed my own light.

VAMPIRES

There are also what I call the "vampire" partners; the type that take a lot and give almost nothing back. Here go some examples:

"Energy vampire"	someone who sucks your energy
"Pessimistic vampire"	someone who takes away your optimism
"Financial vampire"	someone who takes advantage of your money, house, or assets.
"Time vampire"	someone who takes up all your time with his/her demands.

WORTH

We all make some adjustments in relationships, but if you have to compromise your core values and principles to "fit in", this is a very serious red flag.

INSTABILITY

Some people are "moody"; you never know in what mood they will be, so we keep walking on eggshells. Others are "short tempered"; almost anything can take their peace and happiness away. Others are "volatile"; anything can be a reason to break up the relationship at a minute's notice.

MANIPULATION

Consciously or unconsciously humans prey on the weak and often we manipulate others for self-interest, or we let others manipulate us. Either way can be dangerous for a healthy partnership.

EXCHANGE

Be careful! There are "Takers" and "Givers" in this life, and sometimes there are some "Swingers". In my first marriage, the husband was a "Taker" and the wife was a "Giver". He took everything all the time and gave nothing in return, so in the end I was completed drained physically, mentally, emotionally, and financially, which threw me into a very dark depression hole. Thank Goddess I came out of it in just 4 months. Phew!

BOUNDARIES

To love is to live and forgive, but true love can not be blind. To set boundaries and knowing your bottom line is essential for creating a healthy partnership. It's important to know what you will not tolerate in a partner and make it clear from the very beginning, as well as make sure it's clear what would be the consequences of breaking important agreements, like sleeping with someone, etc.

CHECKING YOUR SYNERGY

When I met my Vikingtastic Partner online, we were in completely opposite sides of the planet. I was in New York, USA, and he was in Melbourne, Australia. We could not be more far apart. For me it was essential to meet in person as soon as possible. After our amazing 12-HOUR conversation we kept talking every day for hours.

Thank Goddess for Skype; otherwise we would both have gone broke on the first month, paying for phone calls. It was clear that we were both completely into each other, so I told Ulf that even though I was enjoying our daily virtual talks tremendously, I would only consider this relationship real if we saw each other in person within a month from our first conversation. I know, I could scare him off, but guess what? That is what I wanted and I had no problem saying it. Otherwise it would not work for me.

I was clear also that I had just finished a round the world trip where I spent all my money and at that time I was at home looking for a job. So basically I said: I have time to visit you, but I have no money to travel to the other side of the planet. He said he had no time and no money because he just paid and started his masters degree in Melbourne.

"MariLiza, I like you so much already that I would be willing to wait for you for one year, until you can come to Australia."

"That's so sweet Ulf, but I will be honest with you. As much as you seem to be a fantastic partner for me, I'm not willing to wait for anyone anymore. I don't want a long distance relationship."

Firmly and calmly I continued:
"I don't know how, but we have to find a way to see each other within a month otherwise I don't think this is going to work out for me." On the screen he was a picture perfect man, but who knows when we see each other in person what he would be like. Two weeks into our "many hours" daily conversations, he surprised me with the news that he sold his family's jewelry that he had inherited and he had the money to buy my ticket to go to Australia

to meet him in person. WOW! Not only was he very generous, but he also trusted me by sending the money to my account, so I could choose the airline, buy the ticket and keep the mileage. What planet is he from? The more I got to know this "out of this world" MAN, the more I could not believe how lucky I was — but so was *he*. ;-)

The synergy was flowing in the right direction, and we were both making efforts. I would give my time and effort to travel to the other side of the planet, which I had already done twice before. He was giving his money and effort to accommodate me in his home for one month.

The Synergy was going pretty damn well: mutual excitement, mutual efforts, mutual commitment. So the only last thing to say in this phase was:

"Australia, here I come!"
Wohoooo!

**Does your partnership bring
the best or the worst out of you?**

THE SYNERGY

As my trade mark is to empower the synergy of our most powerful sources — Magic & Logic — when achieving goals, I recommend to apply the dual power to materialize your ideal partner as well. So let's use magic (intuition) and logic (reason) to materialize every stage of a healthy partnership. Some questions can be "out there", but they will help you evaluate the quality of the synergy of your partnership. Take the quiz periodically to check the quality of your new partnership.

1. FEELINGS
How does this partnership make you feel?
Happy? Energized? Inspired? Loved? Friendship?

2. ENERGY
How is your energy when your are around or connected with this partner?
Light? Bright? Expanded? Drained?

3. UNION
Are you great together?
Do you feel better together or apart?
Does this partnership bring the best out of you?

4. HONESTY
Can you be completely honest with your partner?
Even if you have something difficult or unpleasant to say?

5. GROWTH
Are you both growing in great ways?
Are you both more loving because of your time together?
More caring? More open?
Wiser?
Happier?

217

6. AUTHENTICITY

Does your partner love you the way you are?
Do you feel that you can be yourself completely, and not who she/he thinks you should be?

Do you have to change to be "good enough" for this partner?

Do you ever have the sense that you are being manipulated?

7. COMFORT

Are you comfortable with each other physically?
Is sex satisfying for both? Do you enjoy exploring your sexuality as a couple?

Do you feel less like yourself around this partner?

Do you feel that you have to walk on eggshells?

8. AFFILIATIONS

How is your partner fitting in with your family and friends?
Are you happy with your partner's family & friends as well?

9. MATCH

Are you a good match?
Do you feel that you complement each other in outlook, taste, energy?

10. TERMS

Will this partnership make both happy in the short term & long term?
Can you see a positive future with this partner?

"Some partnerships bring

the worst out of us.

Some partnerships bring

the best out of us.

It is up to us to choose."

Prosperous Partnership at Prospect Park
Brooklyn, New York, USA

**Asking each other every year
if we want to be together for one more year.**

THE MATERIALIZATION

After a wonderful month with Ulf in Melbourne, Australia, we knew we wanted to be with each other and date in the same city at least. I was already planning to move to Australia, but it would take one year to get the immigration process done. If I stayed in Australia as a tourist, my visa would eventually expire and I could not work there. Ulf had just started his expensive master degree and loved Australia.

Once again, calmly but firmly I said:
"Now that we both want to be together, let's find a way to live in the same city within 3 months, because as you know I don't want a long distance relationship."

This was no ordinary task for either of us. I laid down the options on the table for us to be together within 3 months:
1. I could go to Australia with my tourist visa, try to work "off the radar", then stay illegally after my visa expired, or
2. I could marry Ulf "on paper" just to be able to stay in the country under his student visa and be able to work, or
3. Ulf could give up everything — school, country, job, friends — and move to the USA.

Even though Ulf had been living for 6 years in Australia, all this time he only had a student visa. First for his Bachelor degree, then for his Honours degree, and later for his Master degree. So once he finished his Master, his visa would expire. He hoped that after his Master degree he could find a job in a company that would sponsor his working visa. At that point, I was already planning to move to Australia anyway, so I thought the "easiest" option was to marry Ulf on "paper" so I could stay in the country and work for as long as his visa lasted. After a year or so together we could decide what to do next. I explained to Ulf that if we "married on paper" it would not be a real marriage for me, just a means to an end. Neither of us was emotionally "there" yet. It would just be a way to be together to date and get to know each other.

Ulf — being a very good boy, never married, who does things by the book — he didn't like that option at all. He said that whenever he decided to get married, he would want it to be for real. So the next option would be for me to go for a few months as a tourist, but that could jeopardize my immigration process in Australia, and I would be doing all the "heavy lifting" of our relationship alone. I didn't consider the last option viable because I knew how much Ulf loved to live in Australia. I knew how much work he had to go through to get his last visa and how much he had compromised financially and emotionally to stay in Australia. I felt that we were in a deadlock, but once again my Vikingtastic partner came around to surprise me big time.

"MariLiza, I love you and I am ready to leave everything behind to be with you anywhere. I can start a new master degree in the US so we can be together."

WOW! OMGG! That amazing revelation knocked me out in the best way possible. Not only was it the first time he said "I LOVE YOU", but he was already committed to leave everything he loved and worked so hard to have just to have a chance to date me. Where is this incredible MAN from again? He must be from another planet visiting Earth disguised as a Handsome Swede.
"MariLiza, if you like and accept this option I promise you that I will be in New York to spend Christmas with you."

Ulf had lived a comfortable life in Melbourne, in a nice

neighborhood next to a gorgeous park, and in a huge house: 3 bedrooms, 2 bathrooms, 2 living rooms, big kitchen, office, backyard, front yard, gym, garage for 2 cars, car, deck and the house even had a beautiful bird nest with lots of baby birds in one of the trees in the backyard. Yes! A great place to live, yet he was ready to give it all up to live with me in my one bedroom apartment in New York where he didn't know anybody and where he never desired to live. Unbelievable! Unfortunately, to add to the challenges, I had to tell him that as my apartment is small, he could only bring some clothes in 2 pieces of luggage because there was no room for anything else in my apartment. He didn't mind!

As crazy as it sounds, in less than 3 months he changed his life completely and got rid of his beloved abundant life in Melbourne. He loved his collections of hundreds of books and videos, but he managed to sell or give them to charity, sold his car, quit his job, cancelled his degree, researched Universities for his multi-media master degree in New York, and managed to be accepted in a very short time, and applied for a student visa at the US embassy.

As I was already back in New York, I couldn't help him with anything, but he never complained about doing all the "heavy lifting". He arrived on Dec/23/2009; just in time for Christmas, without knowing that he made my wish come true: to have my ideal partner living with me by Dec/31/2009. Incredible! Wohooooooooo! THANKS MY DEAR GODDESS for letting me materialize my ideal partner!

After almost two years dating and living together happy, we got married on the cabalistic 11/11/11. A year later, on 12/12/12 we gave birth to our first "baby" book: *WITCH BEAUTY - 10 Secrets for Beauty Transformation*.

Witch Beauty is my true story & strategies, and Ulf's amazing designs & production. It's the first fruit of our love partnership with the purpose of helping more people to feel beautiful in any age, size or shape.

Now we are giving birth to our second baby book, *WITCH PARTNER* to bestow onto others our blessing and help more people to materialize their ideal partner for love, business or other partnership desired.

Life is wonderful, and even better with your ideal partner.

"Whatever You wish...

It's possible,

You can do it,

&

You deserve it!"

**BELIEVING IT'S POSSIBLE,
BEHAVING AS IF IT ALREADY EXISTS
&
BESTOWING THE FRUITS OF IT!**

THE ENHANCEMENT

I've always loved logic and math, so my choice to be a Systems Analyst was no surprise. One of the things we have to be good at as Systems Analysts is to predict all types of things that can go right and go wrong at every stage of a computer system. We predict the possible flaws and force the flaws to happen at the test phase as many times as possible before the system is released. So I had to think ahead of time, as if I was testing one of my computer systems in Wall Street, to come up with all possible things that could go wrong in my partnership plan before they start to happen. In this case, I thought about some of the challenges I could have while materializing my ideal partner:

> What if you have doubts?
> What if it's taking too long to see results?
> What if you don't reach your desired deadline?
> What if you are not 100% sure it will happen?
> What if you are not sure your partner is your ideal?

I know! Been there, and asked those questions myself! Those doubts can arise and they certainly did to me, so I took a deep breath to come back to here, now where everything is just fine. Worries are either in the past or in the future; not in the present.

When we worry, it's like we are praying for what we don't want. Right here, right now, everything is fine. Breathe deeply, paying attention to your breath and then go back to the basics. Evaluate the steps and your commitment to your P3 Plan and keep going.

Things you can modify and test the results:

● TIME FRAME

Change your time frame if you feel like it. Sometimes you are so eager to have something soon that you keep looking at the watch all the time and it shows doubt and insecurity, which definitely keep your dreams at bay.

● APPROACH

If you are not getting the results you want, change something: places you go, people you hang out with, try something new. Then evaluate the results on your self-esteem and on your plan.

● MIND FRAME

Are you behaving as if you already have your ideal partner? Why not? Your vibration of love and gratitude are the "magical dust" that makes dreams come true. Forgive yourself, your past and your past partners.

● RITUALS

Create easy daily rituals to help you keep a healthy self-love and gratitude. Count your blessings daily and say it out loud so you can hear your own voice, and empower your gratitude.

● TRUST & DETACH

Your life is sacred and has a divine purpose. Find and focus on your purpose in life. Live in your heart with the best partner ever: LOVE & GRATITUDE. Be grateful for your life and for all the partners along the way (ideal or not). Pray with gratitude (as if you already have it all) and detachment (as if your happiness doesn't depend on anyone or anything) when asking for your ideal partner. Let your Higher source guide you to the best option for the good of all. Whether you have your ideal partner or not should not keep you from making your dreams come true, from being happy, and from fulfilling your divine mission in this world.

PARTNERSHIP CHECK LIST

Before starting outer procedures, first start with your inner process.

• CHECK CLEANNESS
Have you forgiven yourself and past choices?
Have you forgiven past situations and partners?
Do you count your blessings daily?
Have you acknowledged what you learned from past relationships?

• CHECK SELF-KNOWLEDGE
Do you love yourself?
Do you respect yourself?
What archetype best represents you?

• CHECK BELIEFS
Do you believe it's possible to find your ideal partner?
Do you believe you can manifest your ideal partner?
Do you believe you deserve to find, attract and maintain your ideal partner?
Do you believe every relationship you have is sacred and worth it?

• CHECK CLARITY
Do you have a clear idea about your ideal partner?
Do you have your ideal partner map?
Do you know your Ideal partnership?

• CHECK THE PLAN
What are your daily habits to manifest your ideal partner?
Do you know your allies and aliens?
What are your strategies when faced with temptations to accept less than you deserve?

• CHECK FEEDBACK

Are you checking your efforts and results?

What are you learning in this process?

Do you know how to say "Hello Sunshine" & "Golden Bye"?

• CHECK GRATITUDE

Are you happy with your life?

Are you proud of your mission in life?

Are you building the legacy you desire?

What is your daily gratitude level?

"Live in your heart

with

the best partnership ever:

LOVE & GRATITUDE."

In the math of great partnerships:

1 + 1 = 3

THE TRINITY PARTNERSHIP PLAN

THE P3 PLAN

It's time to put together all the 3 parts of your P3 plan:

THE PERSONA – The Sacred Temple

1. THE PATTERNS – The structures of your Temple
Create your Partners Timeline and identify:
- "Vicious" cycles,
- Ineffective patterns,
- Types of partners

**2. THE PLEASURES – The entertainment
at the Temple**
Identify the different levels of pleasure in your life
and how often you have them:
- Environments,
- Behaviors,
- Capacities,
- Beliefs,
- Identity,
- Affiliations,
- Spirituality.

3. THE POWER – The control of the Temple
Identify the level of control influenced by parts of your life:
- Family,
- Friends,
- Religion,
- Work,
- Society.

4. THE LOVE – The care for the Temple
Score (0=lowest, 10=highest) your current level of:
• Self-awareness, and
• Self-love.

5. THE FREEDOM – The rights in the Temple
Check the state of your authentic "voice":
• Freedom to speak from your true self, and
• Respect and listen to other perspectives

6. THE AFFILIATIONS - The public of the Temple
Check your inner and outer connections and whether your chosen crowds are crowding your path or supporting your journey. To materialize your ideal partner, identify in your journey who are the:
• Aliens
• Allies

7. THE SPIRITUALITY – The purpose of the Temple
Check the purpose of your life by connecting with your higher self or spiritual connection. Define your:
• Vision   What do you want to see in the world?
• Mission   What is your contribution to your vision?
• Values   What guide you through your mission?
• Goals   What steps are you going to take to
                accomplish your mission?

THE PARTNER – The Special Guest

1. THE MENTALISM – The place where it all starts
Design in your mind, and later on paper, your ideal
BETTER approach
• Gratitude
• Recognition
• Materialization
• Experimentation

S.M.A.R.T.E.R. partner
- **S**pecific
- **M**easurable
- **A**ttainable
- **R**elevant
- **T**imely
- **E**cologic
- **R**esources

WISER Belief
Choose to believe in what empowers your goal

2. THE CORRESPONDENCE – The dimensions that matter
Identify the important dimensions of your ideal partner:
- Physical,
- Mental
- Emotional
- Spiritual
- Other (add more if necessary)
- Add the dimensions you considered important to the "Specific" item on your S.M.A.R.T.E.R. Partner description (defined previously in the chapter called "The Mentalism")

3. THE VIBRATION
Identify the time & space for your partner:
- Time outside for trying new places, things and people
- Time inside for visualizing your partner
- Space inside

Does your home have a balanced Yin & Yang energy?
Is there space for your new partner in your home?
- Space outside

What are your passions?
What places fire up your passions?

4. THE POLARITY
Identify the archetype that best represents:
- Your personal identity
- Your last partner's identity
- Your best ex-partner's identity
- Your ideal partner's identity

5. THE RHYTHM
Identify from your partners timeline
- Your effective and ineffective patterns
- The rhythm and frequency of the patterns in your life

6. THE CAUSE & EFFECT
Identify and practice your gratitude about:
- The blessings in your life
- The blessings of having people and partners in your life
- The blessings left by the people who crossed your path

7. THE GENDER
Identify the Yin & Yang energies (feminine & masculine) in your personality and life and check if they are accepted and flowing naturally.

THE PARTNERSHIP – The Mutual Agreement

1.   THE PROACTIVITY
Based on your desired vision, mission, values and goals, add actions to manifest your ideal partner
- Daily proclamations
- Weekly transformations
- Monthly materializations
- Quarterly interactions
- Yearly evaluations

2. THE EXTREMES

Identify in your life:
- The phases of relationships from start to end.
- The examples of relationships in your life with a good beginning & a good ending
- The Practice of acceptance and gratitude toward relationships that ended or changed.

3. THE PRIORITIES

Create a weekly time management:
- Identify your roles in life
- Select your goals
- Schedule your actions

4. THE BENEFITS

Identify the type or interactions you have in your life:
- Lose/Lose nobody benefits from the partnership
- Win/Lose only one benefits from the partnership
- Win/Win both benefit from the partnership

5. THE COMMUNICATION

Identify myths and expectations about relationships:
- Love
- Duty
- Proportion
- Consistency
- Assumption
- Forever
- Turbulence
- Interdependency

6. THE SYNERGY
Check the quality of your relationship periodically and tweak when necessary:
- Feelings
- Energy
- Union
- Honesty
- Growth
- Authenticity
- Comfort
- Affiliations
- Math
- Terms

7. THE ENHANCEMENT
Whether having or materializing your ideal partner, keep paying attention to the overall performance and consistently enhance in any way possible.
When in doubt, go back to the basics:
- Cleanness
- Self-knowledge
- Beliefs
- Clarity
- Plan
- Feedback
- Gratitude

Plan to spend 30 minutes daily investing in your P3 plan:

• 1st month focus on your PERSONA – The temple

Self awareness - Explore the 7 layers of your sacred
temple
Enjoy your own temple (company) – do things
  on your own by choice, not by chance.
Choose a specific time every day to spend
  30 min exploring and expanding your temple.

Example:

      10 min meditating with gratitude.

      20 min trying new things with excitement.

• 2nd month design your ideal PARTNER – The guest

Based on your PERSONA's vision/mission/values/goals
describe your special guest (your ideal partner) and invite
him/her to join your temple (you).
Define when you want to materialize your partner (DD/
MM/YY), when you are going to design your P3 plan and
when you are going to consistently start working on it.
Keep using your 30 min daily, add the visualization.
Example:

      10 min meditating with gratitude

      10 min visualizing your ideal partner

        with your 5 senses

      10 min exploring new places that fire you up

- **3rd month manifest your PARTNERSHIP –
  The agreement**

Live as if you already have your ideal partner
(visualize and talk to him/her in your mind daily, and count
your daily blessings)
Love as you already live the life of your dreams
(do everything you want with or without your ideal partner
and appreciate all the people who cross your path)
Labor the fruits of your partnership to the world (even
when your ideal partner is not there yet)
Start paying attention and making notes of the results
of your state of mind and actions. Evaluate results and
enhance performance. Example:

      10 min meditating with gratitude
      10 min visualizing your ideal partner
        with your 5 senses
      10 min evaluate your journey to move
        toward your desired vision/mission/values/goals

It may sound very little to spend only 30 min per day on
materializing your ideal partner, but the most important
thing is to be consistent with your plan. It's better to start
small and grow from there, than trying to do it all at once
and stop half way. Incorporate and keep in your daily
health routine little steps to materialize your ideal partner,
and you will see remarkable differences.

Witch Partner's Trinity Partnership Plan is meant to be
customized to your aspirations and inspirations. We are
all unique, and so is every P3 Plan. Try new beliefs and
behaviors and see the results. Keep what works best and
keep trying new things. Most of all enjoy the process. Each
partnership, no matter how long or short, is a blessing, an
opportunity to grow. Make the best of it!

"Live as if you already love.

Love as if you already live."

The Partnership.

THE GRATITUDE

THANKS DIVINE GODDESS

For blessing us every day with LILOLA (Light, Love & Laughter) and for granting our wishes to meet each other to materialize our loving partnership.

THANKS VIKINGTASTIC ULF

For being such a loving partner and amazing producer. Without your love, my life wouldn't be as wonderful, and this book wouldn't be a reality. Your creative designs brightened the story and your fantastic production made it come to life. My life is great, and even better with you in it.

THANK YOU

For supporting us along the way with so much love and care. It means the world to us. May your journey be always blessed with lots of great partners in your personal and professional life.

243

They told me, I could not fly … then I rose.
They told me, I was too old … then I was reborn.
They told me, It was impossible … then I made it possible.
They told me, I would fail … then I succeeded.
They told me, I could not be … then I became.

And you can, too, three, four & much more.

It's possible! You can do it & You deserve it!
BE YOU TILL FULL!

Grace & Gratitude,

MariLiza

THE AUTHOR

MARILIZA BACKSTROM

A former Wall Street Systems Analyst, MariLiza worked with the biggest banks in Brazil, UK, and USA. At the top of her career in New York, MariLiza made a radical career change to embrace her greatest passion: helping people make dreams come true.

She became a Coach Master. Since then, she is internationally respected as a Transformation Master, coaching people and companies worldwide. Her successful seminars have been presented in 11 countries, and every year she is invited to work in North America, South America and Europe.

MariLiza stands out with contagious enthusiasm and innovation. The audiences are enchanted by her MAGIC & LOGIC strategies. She continuously researches worldwide to facilitate transformation and maximize results by integrating The Right & The Left hemispheres of the brain.

Her personal mantra is:
BELIEVE wisely, BEHAVE wholly & BESTOW worldwide.

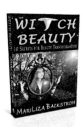

ALSO BY MARILIZA BACKSTROM

WITCH BEAUTY - 10 Secrets for Beauty Transformation

A true story of struggles & strategies from beauty victim to beauty victory. MariLiza's mission in Witch Beauty is to boost self-esteem worldwide, so more people can feel beautiful in any age, size or shape.